Howard Hawks

Robin Wood

London

Secker & Warburg in association with the
British Film Institute

The Cinema One Series is published by
Martin Secker & Warburg Limited
14 Carlisle Street, London W1
in association with *Sight and Sound*
and the Education Department of the
British Film Institute, 81 Dean Street London W1

General Editors
Penelope Houston and Tom Milne (*Sight and Sound*)
Peter Wollen (Education Department)

Howard Hawks by Robin Wood
first published by Martin Secker & Warburg 1968
is a publication of the British Film Institute
Education Department
Copyright © Robin Wood 1968

S B N 436 09863 6 (hardcover)
436 09856 3 (paperback)

Designed by Farrell/Wade

Printed in Great Britain by
Jarrold and Sons Limited Norwich

Contents

Cover: Hawks and John Wayne on the set of *El Dorado*

1: Introduction

There is a tendency to make the distinction between 'art' and 'entertainment' too rigid: the terms are even used as if they referred to directly opposed, mutually exclusive phenomena. Any attempt to define either will show the absurdity of this. If we define 'entertainment' as something that engages and holds the recipient's attention, then what are we to say of a work of art that isn't entertaining? On the other hand the only *essential* factor that distinguishes art from non-art is the artist's personal involvement in his material; if we limit 'entertainment' (in order to keep it distinct from art) to work that shows no involvement at all—no joy on the artist's part in the act of creation—then we are left with only the very lowest commercial products. Obviously, however, the two terms are neither meaningless nor synonymous. A work is 'entertaining' in so far as we spontaneously enjoy it and 'art' in so far as it makes intellectual and emotional demands on us. And one can see that there *could* be a partial conflict between the two: one could name works which demand a deliberate effort of assimilation *before* we can be 'entertained' by them. The examples that spring to mind are mainly contemporary, or at least twentieth-century, works; there is no *necessary* conflict. Many of Mozart's Divertimenti and Serenades were composed for social gatherings at which the listeners wandered about and conversed during the music: 'art' or 'entertainment'? And it's easy to pass from there to Mozart's operas—one of the peaks of European art—and ask the

7

Eldorado: J. P. Harrah (Robert Mitchum) and Cole Thornton (John Wayne)

same question. One can distinguish broadly (so long as one keeps politics out of it) between 'revolutionary' and 'conservative' art: art that deliberately breaks with the immediate past, inventing entirely new forms and new methods of expression, and art that develops out of the immediate past, using forms and language already evolved. Although such distinctions can never be clear-cut, many of the greatest artists would fall into the latter category —Shakespeare, Bach, Mozart; and the fact that so many twentieth-century artists would fall into the former makes it important that we remember this. The genre movie is obviously (by its very nature) 'conservative' art in this sense; and one of the distinguishing features of 'conservative' art is that it is immediately entertaining: audiences were entertained, from the outset, by Shakespeare's plays and by Mozart's operas, and it was possible for an aria from *The Marriage of Figaro* to catch on instantly as a popular hit. The originality of such works lay not in the evolution of a completely new language, but in the artist's use and development of an already existing one; hence there was common ground, from the outset, between artist and audience, and 'entertainment' could happen spontaneously without the intervention of a lengthy period of assimilation. It is distressing that one should have to remind people that a great work of art can be, at least on certain levels, immediately accessible and pleasurable, but, in the age of Beckett and Burroughs, of *Finnegan's Wake* and *Marienbad*, it has become necessary. We must beware of dismissing Hawks's films because we enjoy them.

The Hollywood cinema represents a kind of art that has largely disappeared: to find anything comparable we have to go back to the Elizabethan drama. No other contemporary art form has been able to speak to all social and intellectual levels simultaneously and show a comparable achievement. There are two great contra-dictory truths about Hollywood, and the difficulty of keeping them in reasonable balance is evidenced by the whole history of film criticism, Anglo-Saxon and French alike: (*a*) Hollywood is the vast commercial machine where box-office considerations corrupt everyone and everything, where untrammelled artistic expression is impossible; and (*b*) Hollywood is a great creative workshop, comparable to Elizabethan London or the Vienna of Mozart, where hundreds of talents have come together to evolve a common language. Hold the two in balance and you see why there are so many interesting Hollywood films, and so few entirely satisfying ones.

Modern art is characterised above all by self-consciousness. To the great artists of the past, art was a natural and spontaneous functioning of the whole man. The significance of a Shakespeare play or of a Mozart opera develops out of the artist's direct involvement with his materials as a natural organic process. The modern artist feels himself to be alone, cut off from the traditions of the past, with which he is forced to manufacture some sort of relationship, cut off from modern society, which he tends to loathe. The result is an extreme and habitual self-consciousness; instead of submitting his will to the creative flow, he uses it to insist on the significance of what he is doing. Consider, as a characteristic modern film, Joseph Losey's *Eve*, a distinguished and powerful work, with its own creative intensity, flawed continually by self-conscious insistence on significance. There is the use of that symbolic mask, beginning with its first appearance in the sequence —one of the worst in the film—with the African dancer in the night-club. One feels an enormous gulf between any actual significance the mask has, and the insistent and obtrusive way in which Losey keeps forcing it on our attention; we are far more aware that he means it to mean something than of any actual meaning. From a love scene on a bed Losey cuts to a fountain gushing. We see a girl lay aside a book as her lover comes in: the camera moves across to a close-up of the book so that we can see that it is a copy of Eliot's poems. There is no objection to characterising the girl by showing her reading Eliot; but why waste a whole camera-movement on it?

This kind of thing is so alien to Hawks that I am almost at a loss to find anything in his films sufficiently like it to make direct comparison possible; but there *is* one such moment in *Red Line 7000*. Julie (Laura Devon), the sheltered younger sister of a

Red Line 7000: 'The bubbles are all gone'

race-team manager, sits waiting for her lover, one of the drivers, who has in fact left her. She waits most of the night, with an opened bottle of champagne on the table before her, and when her brother comes to find her, and tells her he has seen her boy-friend out with other women, she looks at the bottle and murmurs that the bubbles are all gone. It's not a profound bit of symbolism, but the point is that Hawks doesn't treat it as if it were. It arises naturally from the scene, and is not imposed on it from the outside: the champagne bottle, apart from any symbolic meaning, is an integral part of the scene, Julie's remark a perfectly natural one. We are not nudged into exclaiming, 'Ah, a symbol! How significant! How deep!'; the beauty of the scene, a very touching one, arises not from any content that can be intellectualised and removed from the images, but from the very precise timing of the acting and the editing, from gesture, expression, intonation, exchanged glance. This is why (the reader had best be warned now) Hawks is ultimately unanalysable. When I am asked by sceptics why I like a film like *Red Line 7000* I can work out a detailed intellectual explanation—the construction of the film, the interaction of all the parts, is, as so often with Hawks, masterly—but it doesn't really satisfy me. What I really like about *Red Line 7000* is the vital tension that is expressed throughout in the great complex of action, gesture, expression, speech, camera movement, camera placing, and editing, that is cinema: the sense of the film's being the work of a whole man, intuitively and spontaneously, as well as intellectually, alive. Nowhere in Hawks is one aware of 'direction' as something distinct from the presentation of the action; there is no imposed 'style'. His definition of a good director: 'Somebody who doesn't annoy you.'

For Hawks is not really a modern artist in the sense in which I have been using the term. He is a survivor from the past, whose work has never been afflicted with this disease of self-consciousness. An artist like Hawks can only exist within a strong and vital tradition, and the weaknesses and limitations of his work are largely determined by those of the tradition that evolved him. On one level, his lack of originality is quite staggering. In a career spanning (so far) over forty years, he has given to the cinema not a single innovation (unless you count the overlapping dialogue technique developed in certain of his comedies). Nearly all his best films are examples of established Hollywood genres, and in virtually every case the genre was fully established before Hawks's film was made. Thus *Only Angels Have Wings* came towards the end of a whole series of films about civil aviation, and has many forerunners which offer close parallels to the characters and situations of Hawks's film—John Ford's *Air Mail* is among the most distinguished. *The Big Sleep* was not the first forties-style gangster film: the innovator was John Huston with *The Maltese Falcon*. *Scarface* followed William Wellman's *Public Enemy*. *His Girl Friday* was a remake of Lewis Milestone's *The Front Page*. *To Have and Have Not* perhaps owes more to Michael Curtiz's *Casablanca* than to Ernest Hemingway. *Rio Bravo*—we have it on Hawks's authority—originated in Hawks's reaction against Fred Zinnemann's *High Noon*; but it is also a Western in the genre which *High Noon* (and before it Henry King's *The Gunfighter*) had established.

A moment's reflection should be sufficient to convince anyone that the existence of established genres is enormously beneficial to the artist and that almost all the greatest art has been built upon the strong and familiar foundations of a genre: Shakespeare's plays, Mozart's symphonies, and Renaissance painting offer obvious parallels. Of course, what we ultimately value in Mozart and Shakespeare are great personal qualities; the genre does not create these, but it does provide a means whereby they can find the fullest and freest expression. The genre-less artist is in fact less free, because he is continually preoccupied with the problems of inventing his own framework, a task which makes, among other things, for extreme self-consciousness. Why does Stravinsky's achievement strike us, in the end, as so inferior to Mozart's? Not necessarily because of any *personal* deficiencies, but because Stravinsky has been forced by the circumstances in which he exists to devote most of his extraordinary creative energies to the invention or discovery or resurrection of forms and frameworks: very often, to revivifying a genre (the classical symphony, classical opera) that has gone dead.

Hawks may not have originated any genres, but he has produced probably the best work within each genre he has tackled. He may not be an innovator, but neither is he an imitator. *Only Angels Have Wings* is no more an imitation of Ford's *Air Mail* (for instance) than *Hamlet* is an imitation of *The Spanish Tragedy*. The genre in each case is transformed from within by the personality of the artist, his way of looking at and feeling things. In all cases where Hawks has taken up a genre initiated by another director— even, I must insist, in the case of *The Big Sleep* and *The Maltese Falcon*, though the difference in quality is much less extreme here —Hawks's film does not merely improve on its predecessor in technical proficiency and general know-how: it is invariably the richer, denser, more personal work, and the earlier work looks thin beside it. More personal: that is the point. A corollary of it is that one does not really think of classifying Hawks's work according to genres. *Rio Bravo* may belong, superficially, in the same genre as *High Noon*, but it has far more in common with *Only Angels Have Wings* and *To Have and Have Not* (and even with *I Was a Male War Bride*) than with Zinnemann's picture; and more in common with them than with Hawks's other Westerns.

Hawks's adjustment to the Hollywood environment has betrayed remarkably few signs of tensions unassimilable into the wholeness of artistic expression. The factors that made this adjustment possible are basic to his art. Before he came to films he flew aeroplanes and drove racing-cars, and he has maintained such interests throughout his life. This has directed his attention naturally to the kind of characters and the kind of milieus most readily compatible with the demands of the box-office. There is no sense anywhere in his work that box-office considerations have compelled him against his will to make films about flying, motor-racing, cattle-driving, or animal-hunting: it is a matter of a most happy coincidence. But there is more to the matter than that. Nowhere in Hawks's work does he show any interest in Ideas, abstracted from character, action, and situation: he has never evinced any desire to make a film on a given moral or social theme. He has always been quite free of the kind of ambitions or pretensions that most often bring directors into conflict with the commercial interests of production companies. The significance of his films never arises from the conscious treatment of a Subject.

Hawks's method of work is firmly and consistently concrete. He starts always from the desire to tell a story. His raw materials are not only the story and the characters, but also the players. Dialogue and situation are often modified during filming as the personality of the actor becomes fused with the character he is playing. Thus the true significance of a Hawks film is not something that could exist on paper before the shooting. The final credit on the films he produces as well as directs frequently reverses the usual wording to read 'Directed and Produced by Howard Hawks'; sometimes the word 'Directed' is given the prominence of larger lettering. A small point in itself, but it indicates where, for Hawks, the creation of a film really lies: neither in the preparation of the

Bringing Up Baby: Cary Grant as David Huxley

script (as with Hitchcock, if we are to believe his repeated insistence that for him the film is virtually completed before shooting begins, with the finalising of the shooting script), nor in the cutting-room (as with Welles), but in the collaboration with actors and cameras that constitutes *mise-en-scène*: a concrete and practical art. His relationship to his actors is at the furthest remove from Josef von Sternberg's. Sternberg regards his actors as 'puppets', it is well known; Hawks regards them as human beings, and works with them in creative collaboration. One begins to understand the nature of his art when one grasps how important to the success of a film is his relationship with its stars. It is in Hawks's films that certain of Hollywood's greatest stars (Cary Grant, Humphrey Bogart, John Wayne) have achieved the completest self-expression without ever leaving us with the sense that the film has been merely a 'vehicle' for them.

All this finally undercuts a recurring objection raised against those critics who take Hawks more seriously than he takes himself.

For he doesn't take his films 'seriously': in interviews, he never speaks of them in terms of 'art', always in terms of 'entertainment'. Characteristically, he speaks of film-making as 'having fun': he and his actors 'had fun' with a certain character or situation. The term points to the one quality essential to a definition of art—the artist's personal involvement, his delight in the creative act; but the way in which Hawks uses it suggests involvement of a not very intense kind. It is never in doubt whom he makes his films for: himself and the mass audience, not 'intellectual' critics. He seems unaware that people are likely to look at his *œuvre* as a whole: his readiness to imitate himself and repeat effects, sometimes after a gap of many years, sometimes after a few, surely implies that he doesn't expect audiences to remember the original. He remarked to Peter Bogdanovich in a television interview, 'When you find out a thing goes pretty well, you might as well do it again': part of the meaning of 'goes pretty well' is clearly 'succeeds with audiences', though it means more than this too. He seemed surprised, when I met him, to learn that I see his films more than once. There is no denying, I think, that this attitude, although inextricably bound up with the kind of artist he is and therefore with his great qualities, has had a detrimental effect on his work. It is not just that some of the imitations are so inferior: in *Man's Favourite Sport?* the night-club bit from *Bringing up Baby*, with the 'love impulse expresses itself in terms of conflict' dialogue; in *Hatari!* the piano-playing bit from *Only Angels Have Wings* ('You'd better be good'). More than that, there is the inescapable sense that Hawks's work doesn't show the degree or consistency of development one finds in the work of the greatest artists. The interrelatedness of Hawks's own limitations and the restrictions imposed by the 'system' is suggested by his remarks (in the same Bogdanovich interview) on why he refused to direct *Fourteen Hours*: he himself 'doesn't like suicides'—he thinks them 'cowardly'; he thinks 'people' don't like them; the film didn't seem as if it were going to be 'any piece of entertainment'. Some remarks on the ending of *Red River* in an earlier interview with Bogdanovich suggest a similar confusion of personal predilection and commercial considerations: 'It frustrates me to start killing people off for no reason at all. I did it in *Dawn Patrol* but when I finished I realised how close I'd come to messing the thing up and I didn't want to monkey with that again. I'm interested in having people go and see the picture, and enjoy it.'

But, although some of the limitations of Hawks's art are suggested well enough by his own attitude to it, its full significance is not. Shakespeare, one guesses, would have spoken of his work in terms of 'art'—a point that suggests something of the gulf that separates his work from that of Hawks; but one feels sure that he would never have explained his work in the sort of terms commonly employed by critics—would have reacted frequently, as does Hawks, by saying something like, 'They attribute things that I hadn't thought of. . . . It's been utterly unconscious.' This does not invalidate critical analysis of his work. The discrepancy between what emerges in the interviews and the claims I (among others) make for Hawks's films can in fact be easily explained by reference to his method of working, his whole concrete and empirical approach to film-making, his intuitive response and spontaneous involvement. If an 'intellectual' film is one in which one senses that the thematic or moral significance was consciously worked out and deliberately expressed, then Hawks is certainly the least intellectual of film-makers. When a masterpiece emerges, it is because Hawks was suddenly completely engaged by his material—not by its significance, intellectually grasped, but by the concrete details of the material itself. When his intuitive consciousness is fully alerted, we get a *Scarface*, a *Rio Bravo*; when it is alerted only spasmodically, we get a *Gentlemen Prefer Blondes* or a *Sergeant York*. Only when his material presents barriers to intuitive involvement and he has to fall back on a conscious mental working-out do we get a downright failure, like *Land of the Pharaohs*.

2: Self-Respect and Responsibility

Only Angels Have Wings (1939), *To Have and Have Not* (1944),
Rio Bravo (1959)

Only Angels Have Wings

Only Angels Have Wings is a completely achieved masterpiece, and
a remarkably *inclusive* film, drawing together the main thematic
threads of Hawks's work in a single complex web.

The opening shots vividly create Barranca, the South American
town in and around which the film is set. The meeting of Bonnie
Lee (Jean Arthur) and Les and Joe, two mailplane pilots (Allyn
Joslyn and Noah Beery, jun.) that inaugurates the action of the
film emphasises their foreignness, and from the moment when they
enter the Dutchman's (Sig Ruman's) saloon the environment is
completely ignored for the rest of the film. From here on, apart
from mailplane flights and the arrival of a boat, we are never off
the Dutchman's premises. Hawks gives us a group sealed off from
the outside world, forming a self-sufficient hermetic society with
its own values. Outside, we are mainly aware of storms, darkness,
and towering, seemingly impassable mountains: only in *The
Thing from Another World* does Hawks again find a setting as ideal
for the expression of his metaphysic.

The film has a wonderful freshness, a total lack of self-
consciousness: no previous film is so inclusive in its exposition of
the director's interests. The method of work is absolutely characteristic: Hawks takes over a genre already firmly established, with
characters who, reduced to their function in the narrative, were
already becoming stock types, and makes it the medium for a

completely personal statement. There is no sign that the director is deliberately rejuvenating a used formula—nowhere does one sense condescension towards the material. There are no intellectual inhibitions about using stock situations or far-fetched coincidences; nor about pushing a scene or a situation through to conclusions many might find excessive, but which are implicit in the material. That Hawks does not feel himself superior to material many may find 'corny', 'melodramatic', or 'banal' is not a sign of inferior intelligence or sensibility. He responds, directly and spontaneously, to all that is valid in the genre, assimilates it and transforms it into a means of personal expression.

The pattern of relationships is complicated; I shall select certain threads that help to make clear the basis of values on which it is constructed. Jeff Carter (Cary Grant) sends men up in all weathers out of loyalty to the Dutchman, flying the plane himself when the weather is too bad to send others. His motivation is primarily self-respect: once a task has been undertaken it must be pursued either to success or to death. To the station comes a flier called Bat (Richard Barthelmess), who once baled out of a blazing plane leaving another to die. He spends his life trying to escape from his own sense of disgrace, reflected in others' reactions: he is motivated by his need to regain self-respect. Jeff's best friend and adorer, Kid (Thomas Mitchell), conceals the fact that his eyesight is failing, because having to give up flying is intolerable to him: flying represents his means of establishing his mastery of things, of preserving the respect of Jeff and hence his self-respect. These three figures constantly recur in Hawks's work; for all three there are ultimately the same values, beyond which there is darkness.

Why do the men fly? Kid tells Bonnie, 'I been in it twenty-two years, Miss Lee. I couldn't give you an answer that makes any sense.' Yeats's Irish Airman was more articulate. After cataloguing, only in order to dismiss, all the accepted reasons for enlisting as a flier in the First World War, he asserted that

> A lonely impulse of delight
> Drove to this tumult in the clouds:

he had summed up past and future and both seemed futile, a 'waste of breath'—all that was real was the impulse, the loneliness, and the tumult, and by those he (briefly) lived. The same desperation underlies the existence of Hawks's fliers; nowhere articulated, everywhere felt.

Attitudes to death are of central importance in *Only Angels Have Wings*. Nowhere in Hawks's later work is this theme so explicit and insistent, though often present. Bonnie Lee, who strongly resembles later Hawks heroines, has in one respect exceptional importance. Bonnie is our means of access, of initiation. Accepting her—for all the unusual nature of her situation—as a representative of our own civilised sensibility, we make our adjustment to the group's code through *her* adjustment, precipitated by the death of Joe, to life lived under the constant shadow of death.

The scene in which the shocked Bonnie watches the reactions of Jeff and the other fliers to Joe's death is justly famous: it generates a terrific intensity. The steaks ordered for Joe's and Bonnie's dinner are served; Jeff takes Joe's. To Bonnie's horrified question as to whether he intends to eat it, Jeff answers, 'What do you want me to do, have it stuffed?' Bonnie, incredulous, tells him it was Joe's. 'Who's Joe?' he asks. Hawks never dwells on the gory details of violent death, but he finds images that make the fact of death disturbingly immediate: the bowling-ball in *Scarface* whose continuing trajectory we watch knowing that the person who cast it is already dead. Here, as Jeff says 'Who's Joe?', we are aware (without the benefit of 'significant' close-ups) of Joe's steak on the plate before him. The tension between Jeff and Bonnie is reflected in the spectator's consciousness. We are, on the whole, identified with Bonnie, sharing her pain and bewilderment at the men's callousness. Yet we know, more than she, that that callousness is more apparent than real, and we are more aware of its necessity. Joe's fatal crash was preceded by the agonisingly tense sequence in which Jeff with his friend Kid's help tried to guide Joe down by radio through a dense fog. We saw the intensity of Jeff's involvement. A successful landing is his responsibility as the head and

Only Angels Have Wings: Bonnie Lee and Jeff Carter

organiser (on the Dutchman's behalf) of the mailplane service: he sent Joe up, insisting on his carrying out his duties: besides, Joe is his friend. The involvement and responsibility underlies and necessitates the brutality: insulation against pain too great to bear rather than cynical tough-mindedness. When the Dutchman expostulates with him about his determination to get the mail out of the wrecked plane and off in another immediately after the crash, Jeff asks if Dutchy thinks he's the only one who cares, then adds, 'Joe died flying, didn't he? Well, that was his job. He just wasn't good enough'—a phrase echoed in many of Hawks's adventure films. 'He'd rather be where he is than quit.' Flying, here, like animal-catching in *Hatari!* or racing in *Red Line 7000*, becomes a means whereby the individual can test himself—a test of character and integrity as much as of skill or physical stamina.

The question of responsibility for the crash adds a further dimension. Part of the responsibility lies with Joe himself: he insists on trying to land, against advice, because he is having dinner with

Bonnie: like Jim Loomis in *Red Line 7000*, he has allowed his feelings for a woman to affect his judgement and lead him into irresponsibility. It constitutes a breach of the professional code, a failure to pass the test, and it is behind Jeff's brutal judgement, 'He just wasn't good enough' (which *doesn't* mean 'sufficiently skilful as a flier'). But the full responsibility is not simply pushed on to Joe. Just before the steak incident Bonnie asks Jeff if it was her fault. 'Sure it was your fault,' he answers. 'You were going to have dinner with him, the Dutchman hired him, I sent him up on schedule, the fog came in, a tree got in the way. All your fault.' The bitter irony points beyond the idea of assignable blame to a complex of circumstances whose interaction at one point in time was unpredictable and uncontrollable. The death was everyone's fault and no one's fault. The characters are denied the comfort of placing the responsibility squarely on one person or one factor. The fliers have to live with this daily. Death may come to us at any minute, but most of us are able to spend most of our lives forgetting this; for the men of *Only Angels Have Wings* there is no forgetting short of a deliberate and extreme rejection: they are constantly exposed to the surrounding darkness. No one who has seen the film will forget Jeff's singing (with Bonnie's participation) of the 'Peanut Vendor', as the culmination of the sequence of Bonnie's initiation into, and acceptance of, the fliers' code. Joe has been dead perhaps an hour. We haven't forgotten, and we know that they haven't. But Joe's death has ceased to be the issue: the song becomes a shout of defiance in the face of the darkness surrounding human life and the chaos of the universe.

This sequence is balanced by the scenes involving the death of Kid. Here the fact of death is brought home to the spectator by Kid's final isolation, under the single light that emphasises the darkness around. He asks for everyone to go until only Jeff is left —and then sends Jeff away too. Ultimately, man is alone; even those close friendships to which Hawks attaches so much importance cease to be of comfort. There follows Jeff's inventory of Kid's belongings, with the comment 'Not much to show for twenty years' flying.' Scene and comment echo a scene earlier, after the death of Joe (and are to be echoed again, most movingly, in *Air Force*), conveying a sense of a stoical ritual. One may recall John Wayne's words over the successive burials in *Red River*: 'We brought nothing into this world, and it's certain we can take nothing out.' Jeff weeps for his friend's death: an acknowledgement of the limitations of the technique of insulation the fliers have evolved—of the ultimate desolation that underlies, somewhere, the warmth, the humour, the affection of Hawks's adventure films—of all that is kept at arm's length by deliberate stoicism.

It is tempting to relate Hawks to existentialism: the existentialist insistence on the need for self-definition—for the establishing, by an act of will, of one's personal identity—has affinities with Hawks's insistence on the need to establish and preserve self-respect. But Hawks is an artist, never a philosopher; he may lead us to certain conclusions through his presentation of an action; but the action is never conceived as illustration of the conclusions, as in Sartre's plays. Compare rather another artist whom existentialists have found interesting: Joseph Conrad. To gauge how extreme are the superficial differences one has only to place *Heart of Darkness* beside *Monkey Business*; yet the same network of interrelated themes underlies the work of both artists.

The scene in *Only Angels Have Wings* where Jeff forces Kid to admit that his eyesight is failing recalls Singleton in *The Nigger of the Narcissus*, where he collapses after his stoical endurance of the storm, and his age is brought home to him for the first time. For both men, the meaning of life has been bound up with a task to be carried out, their means of self-assertion, on which identity depends: and suddenly they are threatened with the removal of the task. Bat, in *Only Angels Have Wings*, is a simplified Lord Jim. The moment in *Rio Bravo* where John Wayne dismisses a gunman set to watch the jail, simply by looking at him and repeating 'Good evening' in a certain tone, calls to mind the scene (*Nigger of the Narcissus* again) in which Captain Allistoun compels Donkin to retrieve and replace the implement flung during the abortive mutiny: in both cases the authority derives from moral integrity, rooted in a firm sense of personal identity—of being committed, ultimately, to certain values. Hawks's interest in the group sometimes recalls Conrad's sea stories (though the cavalry Westerns of Ford, with their intense feeling for tradition, offer closer parallels here): the most striking correspondence is in *Air Force*, where the Mary Ann (the B49) becomes for the crew the unifying symbol and centre of loyalty that the ship is for Conrad's sailors. Hawks's use of certain settings—the Andes in *Only Angels Have Wings*, the Arctic wastes of *The Thing from Another World*— bring to mind Conrad's use of the sea (though, again, Ford's prairie is closer still): it is surprising that Hawks has never made a sea story.

These specific examples indicate a similar implicit metaphysic. Marlow introduces his 'yarn' in *Youth*:

'You fellows know there are those voyages that seem ordered for the illustration of life, that might stand for a symbol of existence. You fight, work, sweat, nearly kill yourself, sometimes do kill yourself, trying to accomplish something —and you can't. Not from any fault of yours. You simply can do nothing, neither great nor little—not a thing in the world—not even . . . get a wretched 600-ton cargo of coal to its port of destination.'

Hawks's heroes usually *do* accomplish the tasks they undertake, yet, though this seems at first an important difference, we are left with a very similar emphasis. If Conrad's heroes fail it is 'not from any fault of theirs'. Actually, in the sea stories, they usually succeed, in the essential of remaining true to themselves—the only *real* failures are like those of Lord Jim, where loss of self-respect, of secure identity, is the penalty. For Hawks's heroes the price of success is often heavy, and the same darkness surrounds their achievements as surrounds the defeat of the characters in Conrad. The value lies, for Hawks as for Conrad, in the assertion of basic human qualities of courage and endurance, the stoical insistence on innate human dignity.

This insistence on 'darkness' and death has been necessary to establish the background to Hawks's art; but no one who has seen *Only Angels Have Wings* will regard it as a gloomy film. Buoyant, vital, exhilarating, are more likely epithets to spring to mind. This tension existing between background and foreground is what gives the most fully characteristic of the adventure films their distinctive flavour. One consistent feature is the positive, dynamic quality of the relationships. It is one of Hawks's greatest strengths—in twentieth-century art a somewhat rare one—that he is able convincingly to portray creative relationships in which the characters help each other, and through which they develop towards a greater maturity, self-reliance, and balance. Is this, rather than the straightforward, functional camera-style and editing, what makes some people regard Hawks's films as old-fashioned? By the end of *Only Angels Have Wings* almost every character has undergone a process of improvement: Bat has re-established himself in the eyes of the other characters and in his own; his wife (Rita Hayworth) has been educated by Jeff—in the most direct way—in her personal responsibilities; Kid has learnt to respect a man for whom he previously felt only contempt (although he has died learning it). Above all, there is the mutual modification of attitude effected between Jeff and Bonny. The film, finally, does not simply uphold Jeff's original attitude. His acceptance of Bonnie, and of the need for feeling and personal commitment even in the sword-of-Damocles world of the fliers, is at least as important as hers of the fliers' code (his breakdown, witnessed by Bonnie, after the death of Kid, is an important stage). The directness—the vital, spontaneous frankness—with which the characters confront and attack each other is enormously affecting, because this urgency of contact derives from their constant (not necessarily conscious) sense of the imminence of death, of the surrounding darkness, a *physical* intuition that prompts them to live, *now*, to the maximum. It is partly this that makes Hawks's films, in fact, so modern: in the world of the hydrogen bomb, one doesn't have to be an Andes mailplane flier to feel that one may be dead tomorrow.

Only Angels Have Wings: Judith, Jeff and Bonnie

To Have and Have Not

To Have and Have Not had an unflattering critical reception in this country in 1945, traceable to three causes. Advance publicity was mostly concerned with selling the new discovery, Lauren Bacall—'Slinky, sultry, sensational'—and determination to appear impervious to indoctrination led many to dismiss Bacall (incredible as it now seems) as a gimmick. There was a feeling that Hemingway's novel had been betrayed (in fact, it is not so much betrayed as ignored—only the first quarter of an hour of the film bears any clear relation to it). Finally, we were too involved in the war to accept—and in a frivolous popular entertainment!—a hero who consistently refused commitment to the right side on the grounds of 'minding his own business', and whose eventual decision to help Free France is primarily motivated by the need to get money to help (*a*) a girl and (*b*) himself, not necessarily in that order. One got the impression from reviews of a thoroughly disreputable film.

To Have and Have Not: Captain Renard, Slim (Lauren Bacall) and Morgan (Humphrey Bogart)

In fact—frivolous popular entertainment or not—*To Have and Have Not* embodies one of the most basic anti-fascist statements the cinema has given us. The sense of moral outrage at the infringement of individual liberty expressed through Bogart's performance is, in its purity and simplicity of feeling, unanswerable: one feels behind it all of Hawks's belief in the individual need for integrity and self-respect.

Bogart is very much the centre of *To Have and Have Not*; the performance is arguably at once the completest realisation of the actor's personality and the most perfect embodiment of the Hawks hero. Hawks always works within a naturalistic framework (everything realised through the details of character and action) but his work shows a continual tendency (favoured and encouraged by the genre system, indeed by the star system itself) to move towards myth. Lorelei and Dorothy in *Gentlemen Prefer Blondes* are more like figures in myth than figures from real life—distillations from essential reality rather than depictions of reality itself.

Hawks's Harry Morgan is really no more a 'real' character than the heroes of Homer, though we accept him as real during our experience of the film just as we accept Homer's heroes as real. Morgan, though entirely unidealistic (and from some points of view unheroic), embodies a certain heroic ideal. Argument must be concerned with the validity of the values it represents.

Morgan persistently rejects commitment, until the time comes when he is directly and personally involved and it is no longer a matter of choice. It would be mistaken to see the subject of the film as the necessity for commitment, although the scenario could be read like that without much wrenching, and doubtless the hero's eventually entering the fray on the right side helped to make the film just acceptable in 1945. But even when he finally joins the fight against fascism (represented mainly by the gross Captain Renard, a superb performance by Dan Seymour), Morgan continues to see things in resolutely personal terms: 'I like you and I don't like them.' The 'I' is all important. Hawks and Bogart give us a man who exists exclusively from his own centre, his actions stemming from the immediate perceptions and impulses of his consciousness. Here the term 'individual' really means something: not merely 'Someone who is different from other people', but 'a conscious being who lives from his own feeling centre of identity'. It is not a question of egotism: Morgan is never self-indulgent, or self-seeking beyond what he defines as his rights. He is a man whose sense of essential responsibility has been remarkably uncorrupted by either materialism or idealism. Morgan acknowledges a certain responsibility to Johnson (Walter Sande), who is hiring both Morgan and his boat; but he sees this as secondary to his responsibility to Eddie (Walter Brennan), the alcoholic hanger-on who 'used to be good', and when the two responsibilities clash there is no question which Morgan puts first. When Captain Renard asks him, 'What are your sympathies?' Morgan replies, in a phrase taken up and developed in *Rio Bravo*, 'Minding my own business'; but his 'own business' includes Eddie and, later, Slim (Bacall)—includes anyone who earns Morgan's respect and *personal* allegiance. Responsibility is for Morgan a matter of instinct, not duty, an impulse of sympathy arising spontaneously from the living centre.

Life lived from a spontaneous-intuitive centre is life without fixed rules. Bogart's character determines the film's flexible and empirical morality. Bacall's theft of Johnson's wallet reveals that Johnson intended to 'skip' without paying Bogart. A rigid morality would insist on the reprehensibility of both actions (the stealing and the skipping). But here actions are referred to what you *are*—there are no rigid moral rules. We watch Bogart confront both Bacall and Johnson with their dishonesty, and we compare the differences in their reactions. Bacall makes no attempt to cover up for herself, refusing to show shame. It was something she was forced to do so she did it—*she*, as a person, remains unaffected. It is the principle of *Vivre sa Vie*, where, we are told, Anna Karina sells her body but preserves her soul: in both cases, a distinction is made between what one *does* and what one *is*, with the implication that it is possible to retain a sense of personal identity which is not contaminated or affected by one's actions if one doesn't let it be. Johnson gets no sympathy at all, again because of what he *is*: confronted with his dishonesty, he bluffs, squirms, loses dignity.

Bogart himself has to learn not to judge from appearances; to learn the dangers of the stock response. He assumes he knows Bacall from the way she took the slap administered by brutish officialdom: 'It takes practice,' he casually comments. She tells him (and Angie Dickinson will echo the words in *Rio Bravo*) that he has made up his mind about her too soon: he must learn, in other words, to see her as an individual, not a type; to see the woman, not the actions. Gradually, beneath her façade of toughness, her vulnerability becomes touchingly apparent. The mask is for the world: beneath it she has preserved her innate sensitivity.

Bogart, like Bacall, is direct and honest about himself. 'You save France,' he tells de Bursac (Walter Molnar), 'I'm going to save my boat.' He is equally direct in his dealings with others. The relationship with Slim develops so rapidly because he lets her know exactly how he thinks about her, and can therefore quickly be proved wrong. He consistently refuses to sympathise with people who ask for sympathy. When Frenchy (Marcel Dalio) tells him plaintively that Madame de Bursac 'is not herself', his instant response is to inquire 'Who is she?' Later Madame apologises for being a trouble. 'You're not sorry at all,' he tells her. 'You're just sorry you made a fool of yourself.' As a result, the woman's self-important superiority breaks down, and the human being beneath it emerges. His treatment of Eddie anticipates Chance's training of Dude in *Rio Bravo*—especially in their confrontation after Eddie has stowed away in the boat. He is worried in case Eddie 'doesn't hold together', and tells him so straight out, withholding sympathy because it would weaken the man. Yet the treatment is not callous: all that Bogart does is done from a responsible concern. This directness comes across, not as any form of self-display, certainly not as an affectation or a tough pose, but simply as the expression of Bogart's individualism. It creates instant antagonisms—he admits to Bacall that most people 'get sore' at him as soon as they meet him—yet it is the quickest way to a true understanding, testing and discovering the other person.

I spoke earlier of an 'anti-fascist statement', using the term 'fascist' somewhat loosely. The protest is against any authoritarian interference with the rights of the individual. Hawks admits to not being very interested in the 'political intrigues', and sees the plot as 'just an excuse for some scenes'. Fair enough. And clearly he sees the scenes in terms of the essential expression of Bogart and Bacall. But it is precisely through them that the basic political statement is made. It is the individualism of Bogart/Morgan that gives such force to moments like the one where Bacall/Slim is slapped in the face. Tremendous moral authority is invested in Bogart in these scenes: the protest of the true individual against the abuses of those in power. Hawks works as Bogart/Morgan works, in absolutely concrete, empirical terms. One never has the feeling that a 'message' is being 'put across': the significance grows spontaneously out of the relationship of director, actor, character, and situation, and has the greater force for doing so: the scenes, like Bogart's actions, become the direct expression of an individual feeling spontaneously from a vital centre. There are, above all, the climactic scenes with Captain Renard. Three points must be mentioned. Firstly, the extraordinary moment when Bogart learns that the police have got Eddie, and he may be being tortured or killed. Earlier, Bacall's façade of toughness crumbled in the stress of her relationship with Bogart. Bogart/Morgan's apparently impregnable self-sufficiency has been preserved till this moment. Suddenly we see Morgan's vulnerability for the first time—the face seems to age before our eyes, its battered, experienced quality suddenly taking on a despair that deepens the significance of all that has gone before by placing it in a new perspective. Secondly, there is the shot fired through the table from the gun in the drawer: one of the finest instances of Hawks's marvellous ability to find an action that expresses the inner emotional quality of a scene. The success of the action (like a similar moment near the end of *The Big Sleep*, or the flower-pot scene in *Rio Bravo*) depends on a spontaneous, split-second timing and the partnership between man and woman. The sudden violence of the bullet ripping through wood to secure the characters' freedom is at once the explosion and the relief of the accumulated tensions of the whole film. Hawks is above all a *physical* director: the cinema is the perfect medium for expressing emotion or moral values through actions. Finally, there is Morgan's beating of Captain Renard: another instance of the film's insistence on moral flexibility. The answering of violence with violence; yet one *feels* the morality of the scene to be impeccable—far more confidently than with a parallel scene in *El Dorado*. The distinction *To Have and Have Not* insists on is that between the application of calculated, official force imposed from above, and the spontaneous expression of the individual's sense of moral outrage: again, the accumulated tensions of the whole film are behind it. It recalls the scene in *Air Force* (made the year before) where Winocki (John Garfield) kills the Japanese fighter pilot.

Bogart and Bacall fell in love during the making of *To Have and Have Not*: impossible to forget this once one knows it. Seldom have two stars played to each other with such spontaneous

precision. I cannot understand why the reputation of this film's companion-piece, *The Big Sleep*, stands so much higher. The dialogue of *The Big Sleep* is consistently slick and clever, that of *To Have and Have Not* is too, but it is given far more edge by our awareness of freer and more powerful emotions underlying it. The world of the later film is much more enclosed, in terms of the range and intensity of feeling possible within it. Whereas *The Big Sleep* is marginal to Hawks's work, *To Have and Have Not* is central to it.

Rio Bravo

The genesis of *Rio Bravo* was Hawks's reaction against *High Noon*: the hero of *High Noon* spends the whole film asking for help and in the end he doesn't need it. Hawks decided to reverse the process: the hero of *Rio Bravo* never asks for help and often rejects it; and he needs it at every crisis. The relationship between the two films is not quite as simple as that; the two exceptions to this general reversal-pattern are interesting, as they may both have suggested to Hawks, whether he was aware of it or not, aspects of *Rio Bravo*: (1) The Marshal (Gary Cooper) in *High Noon does* once reject the help of a one-eyed drunken cripple who sees in his offer of assistance the possibility of regaining his self-respect: 'I used to be good', he tells Cooper, a line doubtless as common in Westerns as certain musical phrases were common in late eighteenth-century music, yet one which Hawks (like Mozart with *his* contemporary clichés) can fill with intensity. Are we to see in this the genesis of Dude and Stumpy? In one way obviously not, because both these characters, and their relation to the film's main hero-figure, have their ancestry in Hawks's own work, notably Eddie in *To Have and Have Not*. Yet, given the admitted relationship of *Rio Bravo* to *High Noon*, and the complexity of influence and reminiscence that can underlie any great work of art, it may not be far-fetched to feel some significance in this passing resemblance. (2) Grace Kelly's final intervention (shooting a man in the back to save her husband, against her Quaker principles) is one point where Cooper *does* need help, and may point forward to *Rio*

Bravo's celebrated flower-pot scene and Angie Dickinson's subsequent distress at having been responsible for the deaths of four men.

The reputation of *High Noon*—it is still widely regarded as one of the best Westerns, a film that confers dignity on a low genre by infusing into it a seriousness of moral purpose—is very revealing, as regards current attitudes to the Western and to film in general. This reputation is my only reason for undertaking a brief comparison of the two films: *High Noon* in itself doesn't offer anything that the critic who regards the cinema as, in its potentialities and to some extent its achievements, the equal of the other arts is likely to find worth serious consideration. It strikes me as the archetypal 'Oscar' film, product of the combined talents of the archetypal 'Oscar' director (Zinnemann), the archetypal 'Oscar' writer (Carl Foreman), and the archetypal 'Oscar' producer (Stanley Kramer): three gentlemen whose work has been characterised by those Good Intentions with which we understand the road to hell to be paved. *Mental* intentions, not emotional or intuitive intentions: intentions of the conscious, willing mind, not of the whole man. The film reeks of contrivance. Every sequence is constructed to lead up to, and make, a simple moral point, character, action, and dialogue being painstakingly manipulated to this end. Nowhere is there that sense of inner logic, of *organic* development, of the working-out of natural processes through the interaction of the characters, that one finds in the best films of Hawks. This characteristic is not only in the script. Zinnemann's direction, external and shallow, matches it perfectly. His handling of the actors is almost uniformly abominable, cliché-gesture following cliché-gesture (see, for instance, poor Thomas Mitchell, whose Kid in *Only Angels Have Wings* is among the American cinema's great supporting performances, in the church scene), just as cliché-set-up follows cliché-set-up in the camera positioning.

Quite fundamental issues are involved here, including the question of what constitutes cliché. But in *High Noon* not a single character or situation is spontaneously-intuitively *felt*—everything is in the head, a painstaking application of carefully learnt lessons. One could attack Carl Foreman's script for its contrivance, but, ultimately, to understand why *High Noon* is a bad film is to understand that the cinema is a director's art. There are situations, such as the scene between Katy Jurado and Lloyd Bridges where her contempt for him finally erupts after long suppression, which are perfectly valid emotionally, but which Zinnemann relentlessly turns into cliché-melodrama with his academically conceived jumps into close-up at the most obvious moments, his insistence on acting that is conventional in the worst sense (it isn't the actors' fault), the obviousness of gesture and expression exactly corresponding to the obviousness of the editing.

Judgements of this kind are notoriously difficult to enforce when dealing with the cinema (how great an advantage the literary critic has in being able to quote!): one has to appeal not only to the reader's common experience, but to his memory of that experience. One can, however, in the case of *High Noon*, point to several obvious major inadequacies which are symptomatic of the quality of the film as a whole—its quality as a work of art, as a record of lived and felt experience (however indirectly expressed). There is the entire church sequence, where the cliché-treatment both of the congregation *en masse* and of individuals reaches risible extremes. There is the handling of the Cooper-Kelly relationship. It is presumably of importance that the audience feel this as meaningful, that a sense of frustrated mutual needs and resulting tensions is communicated. Yet if we look at what Zinnemann actually offers us we find, apart from one or two tentative attempts at inwardness from Grace Kelly in the early stages of the film, nothing at all convincing. The wife remains a mere puppet, manipulated according to the requirements of the plot: no understanding of her reactions is communicated, beyond the explicit statement of her Quakerism, which is then merely taken for granted. Everything important, in fact, is taken for granted: Cooper's need for her, the importance of the marriage to him, is reduced to a bit of data, never *felt* as real. Someone, indeed, seems to have felt that there was something missing there, that the marriage-theme needed a bit of artificial bolstering; hence the tiresome repetition on the soundtrack of the lines from the theme-song, 'I'm not afraid of death but Oh! what will I do if you leave me?'—the importance of the marriage is only there in the song, an explicit statement of intentions that remain quite unrealised.

But most interesting of all, in relation to Hawks and *Rio Bravo*, is the motivation of the hero's actions. It is clear, I think, that for the Marshal, as for Hawks's heroes, the essential motivation is the preservation of self-respect—he goes back to face Frank Miller because a failure to do so would be, for him, a failure to live up to his own conception of manhood. One may reflect that this is a theme that lends itself readily to (could even be said to be implicit in) the Western genre. It is not its theme that makes *Rio Bravo* great, but the intensity and emotional maturity with which it is felt. The level on which the theme is handled in *High Noon* can be, I think, fairly represented by the scene where Grace Kelly confronts Katy Jurado and asks her *why* Cooper is determined to stay. Cut to close-up of Jurado, who says, with heavy emphasis, 'If you don't know, I can't explain it to you.' The reader who doesn't see what I mean by cliché (in terms of acting, editing, camera-position) couldn't do better than study that moment. The reputation of *High Noon* rests, in fact, on two things, both quite superficial in relation to what the film actually *is*: its strict observation of the unities (which it never lets us forget), and its 'Message'. Its message is really its whole *raison d'être*.

Rio Bravo is the most traditional of films. The whole of Hawks is immediately behind it, and the whole tradition of the Western, and behind that is Hollywood itself. If I were asked to choose a film that would justify the existence of Hollywood, I think it would be *Rio Bravo*. Hawks is at his most completely personal and individual when his work is most firmly traditional: the more established the foundations, the freer he feels to be himself. Everything in *Rio Bravo* can be traced back to the Western tradition, yet everything in it is essential Hawks—every character, every situation, every sequence expresses him as surely as every detail in an Antonioni film expresses Antonioni.

List the stock types of Western convention, and your list will almost certainly include the following:

1. Hero: strong, silent, infallible.
2. Hero's friend: flawed, fallible, may let him down or betray him (through cowardice, avarice, etc.).
3. Woman of doubtful virtue, works or sings in saloon, gambles; will probably die saving hero's life.
4. Nice girl, schoolteacher or farmer's daughter, open-air type, public-spirited; will marry hero when he settles down.
5. Hero's comic assistant, talks too much, drinks.
6. Singing cowboy, plays guitar.
7. Comic Mexican, cowardly, talks too much, gesticulates.

In six of these seven stock types we can recognise the basis of the six leading characters of *Rio Bravo*; only the clean-living farmer's daughter is missing. These stock figures are used without the slightest self-consciousness or condescension. Hawks builds on these traditional foundations; he also builds on his actors, exploring and using their particular resources and limitations creatively. Just as *To Have and Have Not* gave us the fullest expression of Bogart, so here John Wayne, Dean Martin, Walter Brennan, and others are able to realise themselves, to fulfil the potentialities of their familiar screen *personae*. The extraordinary thing is that, while they can all be referred back to traditional Western types and to the personalities of the actors, the characters of *Rio Bravo* are at the same time entirely and quintessentially Hawksian, un-mistakable in their behaviour, their attitudes, their dialogue. The film offers, I think, the most complete expression we have had of Hawks himself, the completest statement of his position. There are no clichés in *Rio Bravo*.

The complex flavour of the film can be partly defined in terms of apparent contradictions: it is strongly traditional yet absolutely personal; it is the most natural of Westerns, all the action and interrelationships developing organically from thematic germs that are themselves expressed as actions, yet it is also stylised; if one looks at it dispassionately, one becomes aware of an extreme austerity—a few characters, the barest of settings, no concessions to spectacle (with the exception of the dynamite at the end) or prettiness, yet if one submits to the atmosphere and 'feel' of the film one is chiefly aware of great richness and warmth. These characteristics are all very closely interconnected. It is the traditional qualities of the Western that allow Hawks to make a film so stylised in which we are so little aware, until we stand back and think about it, of stylisation; the stylisation and the austerity are but two ways of naming the same thing; the richness and warmth emanate from Hawks's personality, which pervades the whole; and it is the traditional and stylised form that sets him free to express himself with the minimum of constraint or interference.

The term 'traditional', applied to the Western, can mean two things, and two very different kinds of Western. The genre gives great scope to the director with a feeling for America's past, for the borderline of history and myth, the early stages of civilisation, primitive, precarious, and touching. But the genre also offers a collection of convenient conventions which allow the director to escape from the trammels of contemporary surface reality and the demand for verisimilitude, and express certain fundamental human urges or explore themes personal to him. If the classic Westerns of John Ford, with their loving and nostalgic evocation of the past, are the supreme examples of the first kind, *Rio Bravo* is the supreme example of the second. The distinction, obvious enough yet very important, can be exemplified by comparing the town in Ford's *My Darling Clementine* with the town in *Rio Bravo*. Ford's Tombstone is created in loving detail to convey precisely that sense of primitive civilisation against the vastness and impersonality of nature, the profound respect for human endeavour and human achievement exemplified in even the simplest of men that is so characteristic of this director: on the one hand the Bon Ton Tonsorial Parlour and the honeysuckle-scented hair-spray, the tables in rows neatly laid with cloths in the dim hotel dining-room; on the other, the vast expanses of wilderness from which strange-shaped rocky projections grandly rise. Ford places his community against the wilderness, the wooden hotel, the skeletal wooden church tower, the dancers on the uncovered church floor unselfconsciously enjoying themselves under the sky, surrounded on all sides by the vast emptiness of desert.

There is nothing like this in *Rio Bravo*. Here the whole Ford theme of the defence of civilised order and civilised values against destructive elements is compressed into the single strong reaction evoked so powerfully by the murder, brutal, gratuitous, stupid, that precipitates the entire action. Hawks's town consists of jail, hotel, saloons, and rows of unadorned and inconspicuous house-fronts; inhabitants appear only when the narrative demands their presence, and there is never the least attempt to evoke that sense of community that is one of the finest and most characteristic features of the work of Ford. If a barn contains agricultural implements, they are there to provide cover in a gun-fight, not to suggest a background of agricultural activity; if the barn is littered with dust and straw, this is not to create atmosphere or a sense of place, but simply to use to blind a character momentarily. Every item of décor is strictly functional to the action. The social background is kept to the barest minimum below which we would be *aware* of stylisation. Even the jail and hotel which are the two main centres of the action are not felt as having any real social function (no one seems to stay in the hotel unless the plot requires them: mainly only Angie Dickinson); but there is a certain unobtrusive symbolic opposition between them (women tend to dominate in the hotel, and are excluded from the jail, where a miniature all-male society develops in isolation). The bar in which the action begins is so neutral in atmosphere that it scarcely registers on the spectator as a 'presence': Hawks uses it neither to suggest any potential fineness of civilisation (however primitive) nor to create a background of incipient violence and disorder: it is just a bar. Neither is there any attempt at 'period' evocation: the costumes, while not obtrusively stylised, are quite neutral in effect.

The result of all this is twofold. It frees Hawks from all obligation to fulfil the demands of surface naturalism, the accumulated convention of the Western tradition allowing him the simplest of frameworks which can be taken on trust; and this enables him to concentrate attention on the characters and their relationships, and the characteristic attitudes and themes developed through those relationships, to an extent impossible in an outdoor Western: we feel far more intimate with the characters of *Rio Bravo* than with those of *Red River*, let alone *The Big Sky*. The neutral background of the opening scene throws the initial confrontation between Wayne and Martin into forceful relief. But it would be a mistake to see the stark simplicity of setting in this film as *merely* a convenience. It has also, and more importantly, an expressive function, providing a perfect environment for the stoicism that characterises Hawks's attitude to life. The action of *Rio Bravo* is played out against a background hard and bare, with nothing to distract the individual from working out his essential relationship to life. The virtual removal of a social framework—the relegating of society to the function of a *pretext*—throws all the emphasis on the characters' sense of *self*: on their need to find a sense of purpose and meaning not through allegiance to any developing order, but within themselves, in their own instinctual needs.

The value of existing conventions is that they not only give you a firm basis to build on but arouse expectations in the spectator which can be creatively cheated. We can study this principle in any art form in any period where a highly developed tradition is available to the artist. One can see it very clearly in Mozart: much of the freshness of his music, its ability continually to surprise and stimulate the listener into new awareness, derives from his use of the 'conventional' language of the age in order to arouse and then cheat expectations—from a constant tension between the conventional background and the actual notes written. The effect depends very much on our awareness of the background, which needn't necessarily be a *conscious* awareness. This tension between foreground and background, between the conventions of the Western and what Hawks actually does with them, is everywhere

(Above and opposite) *Rio Bravo:* Chance and Feathers

apparent in *Rio Bravo*. It will be immediately evident, for anyone who has seen the film, in the relationship of the actual characters on whom the film is built to the stereotypes I listed above. Consider, for example, how Hawks uses John Wayne—both his qualities and his limitations. He is the archetypal Western hero, strong, silent, infallible. His taciturnity becomes the occasion for humour (especially in the scenes with Angie Dickinson) which is dependent partly on our awareness of John T. Chance as a genre-character; at the same time, the concept of stoical heroism Wayne embodies provides the film with one of its major touchstones for behaviour. For all the sophistication and the unobtrusive but extreme virtuosity, Hawks's art here has affinities, in its unself-consciousness, its tendency to deal directly with basic human needs, its spontaneous-intuitive freshness, with folk-song: consider, for instance, the refusal to identify most of the characters with anything beyond descriptive-evocative nicknames: Dude, Feathers, Stumpy, Colorado . . . even Chance *sounds* like a nickname.

Colorado has a surname somewhere, but who remembers it? One feels the characters as coming from a folk-ballad rather than from any actual social context: they have that kind of relationship to reality.

Feathers is the product of the union of her basic 'type'—the saloon girl—and the Hawks woman, sturdy and independent yet sensitive and vulnerable, the equal of any man yet not in the least masculine. The tension between background (convention) and foreground (actual character) is nowhere more evident. We are very far here from the brash 'entertainer' with a heart of gold who dies (more often than not) stopping a bullet intended for the hero. Angie Dickinson's marvellous performance gives us the perfect embodiment of the Hawksian woman, intelligent, resilient, and responsive. There is a continual sense of a woman who really grasps what is important to her. One is struck by the beauty of the character, the beauty of a living individual responding spontaneously to every situation from a secure centre of self. It is not so much a matter of characterisation as the communication of a life-quality (a much rarer thing). What one most loves about Hawks, finally, is the aliveness of so many of his people.

Stumpy (Walter Brennan) and Carlos (Pedro Gonzalez-Gonzalez) are brilliant variants on the Western's traditional 'comic relief' stock types. Both are so completely integrated, not only in the action, but in the overall moral pattern, that the term 'comic relief' is ludicrously inadequate to describe their function. With Stumpy, as with Chance/Wayne, the traditional figure merges indistinguishably into the personality of the actor. Brennan's *persona* of garrulous and toothless old cripple has been built up in numerous other films (some of them Hawks's—*To Have and Have Not*, *Red River*). Hawks's method with Brennan/ Stumpy is the same as with Wayne/Chance: the character is pushed to an extreme that verges on parody. With Chance this has the effect of testing the validity of the values the *persona* embodies by exposing them to the possibility of ridicule. With Stumpy the effect is dual: on the one hand we have Brennan's funniest and richest, most completely realised impersonation; on the other, the character's position in the film ceases to be marginal (as 'comic relief' suggests). His garrulity gradually reveals itself as a cover for fear and a sense of inadequacy; it plays an essential part in the development of the action, contributing to Dude's breakdown. With Stumpy, humour and pathos are inseparable. The response the characterisation evokes is remarkably complex: he is funny, pathetic, maddening, often all at the same time; yet, fully aware of his limitations, we never cease to respect him.

Carlos raises a more general problem: what some critics have described as Hawks's racialist tendencies. I feel myself that Hawks is entirely free of racial feeling; with Carlos, with the Dutchman in *Only Angels Have Wings*, with the French-Canadians in *The Big Sky*, he is simply taking over genre-figures (and often the character-actors associated with them) and building on them. One can say that the very existence of such stock figures is itself insulting, and this is fair enough; one can, I suppose, go on from that to complain that Hawks is unthinkingly helping to perpetuate the insult; but that is rather different from finding actual racial malice in his attitude. He is simply—and very characteristically—making use of the conventions (and the actors) that are to hand, and not questioning their initial validity. He takes the stock figure of the comic, cowardly, gesticulating, garrulous Mexican and, by eliminating the cowardliness while playing up the excitability, builds up a character whose dauntlessness and determination win our sympathy and respect even as we laugh at him. Hawks's handling not only revivifies and humanises the stock type, but greatly increases his dignity and (moral!) stature.

But it is the figure of the Hero's Fallible Friend that is most fully worked on and transformed in *Rio Bravo*. Significantly, perhaps, this is the least stereotyped, the most uncertain and unpredictable, of the traditional Western ingredients. What I have in mind, however, is a character the variations on which the reader will have little difficulty in recognising, whose function is usually to act as a foil to the hero, to set off his integrity and incorruptibility. Usually, he falls from grace either through weakness, personal inadequacy, or (more often perhaps) his betrayal of the hero, and gets killed. The characters played by Arthur Kennedy in two of Anthony Mann's excellent Westerns, *Where the River Bends* and *The Man from Laramie*, are interesting variants on the basic type; Lloyd Bridges in *High Noon* is another example. A part of this function—a foil to set off the hero's moral infallibility—is still clearly operative in *Rio Bravo*; but Dude takes on such importance in the film that it becomes a question at times who is a foil for whom. Hawks says *Rio Bravo* is really Dean Martin's picture; and if one disagrees, it's not because it's John Wayne's, but because what gives *Rio Bravo* its beauty is above all the interaction of all the parts, the sense that its significance arises from the ensemble, not from any individual character in isolation. Otherwise Hawks (who said of the ending of *Red River* that he couldn't see the sense of killing people off unnecessarily) exactly reverses the Fallible Friend's usual progress: instead of decline and betrayal, we have a movement (despite setbacks) towards salvation. And it is very important that the first step in that salvation is the mainspring of the film's whole action: it is typical of Hawks that everything should hang, ultimately, on a matter of *personal* responsibility, not social duty.

Rio Bravo, then, is firmly rooted in a certain Hollywood tradition, and awareness of the tradition and its conventions can help to enrich our response to it. Nevertheless, it is equally true to say that the film can be understood without reference to 'the Western' at all. It is as firmly rooted in Hawks's own past. Hawks has never rejected his past, and never really left it behind. In a sense, *Rio Bravo* subsumes almost everything he had done previously (without, of course, making the other films redundant). The expository first few minutes, where the situation from which all the action develops, and the film's central relationship, are established without a word being spoken, constitute, whether intentionally or not, a homage to the silent cinema that takes us right back to Hawks's roots. The whole pattern of relationships in the film will be familiar to those who have seen *Only Angels Have Wings* and *To Have and Have Not*. Consider the following parallels between the three films: the three heroes (Grant, Bogart,

44

Wayne) are all variations on a basic concept; the women (Arthur, Bacall, Dickinson) all share a strong family resemblance, and there are clear similarities in their relationships with the films' respective heroes. Stumpy, obviously, can be traced back to Eddie in *To Have and Have Not*: the fact that both are played by Walter Brennan makes the similarity very conspicuous. But Dude can be traced back to Eddie too, and also to Bat in *Only Angels Have Wings* (one would not readily have connected Bat and Eddie without this sense that they are both partly subsumed in Dude). Stumpy is also related to Kid in *Only Angels Have Wings*—there is the same fear of growing old and no longer being of any use. Carlos has something in common with the Dutchman in *Only Angels Have Wings* and with Frenchy in *To Have and Have Not*; further, the 'responsibility' he is given of putting Feathers on the stagecoach recalls the task of putting Slim on the plane entrusted to Crickett (Hoagy Carmichael). Both fail.

What is important to note are the differences that such juxtapositions force on the attention. The quite different 'feel' of the three films is largely determined by the differences between their heroes. Grant in *Only Angels Have Wings* is much younger than the other two men, and strikes one as essentially more vulnerable (he is I think the only Hawks hero who ever cries), less finally formed by experience, his maturity and balance less secure. Hence the more extreme and drastic—almost exhibitionistic—nature of his rejection of sentimentality: it almost becomes the rejection of feeling itself, a trait criticised and qualified during the film. With the other two, especially Wayne, we are made aware of limitations rather than imperfections. Also, while Wayne and Bogart are both confronted with the *possibility* of their associates' death or collapse, Grant is the only one confronted with death itself. The possibility of desperation, which seems always, almost invisibly, to underlie the good-humoured surface of the adventure films, is much more apparent in *Only Angels Have Wings* than in the later works, and it is largely the nature of the protagonist that makes this possible. Bogart, on the other hand, of the three is the one most completely in command of the situations he finds himself in. Wayne appears to be in command; but a leading point of *Rio Bravo*—it amounts almost to a 'running gag' —is that he isn't: his safety and success depend at every crisis on the timely intervention of others. *To Have and Have Not* and *Rio Bravo* are probably the two Hawks films which are closest to each other (if one excepts *Ball of Fire* and its inferior remake *A Song is Born*): the likeness of *El Dorado* to *Rio Bravo* may be more immediately obvious, but it proves on closer acquaintance also more superficial. *Rio Bravo* and *To Have and Have Not* give us closely parallel patterns of character-relationships, and even stretches (in the Bogart/Bacall and Wayne/Dickinson exchanges) of almost identical dialogue. The real difference between them rests not on obvious differences of location and plot-twists, but on the different relationship of the hero to the total work. In fact, the more one thinks about the three films, the more different they seem.

The wordless first minutes of the film are a good example of Hawks's use of actions to speak for themselves. Why does Dude strike Chance down? Why does Chance, despite his injury, so rashly—on the face of it hopelessly—follow and try to arrest Joe Burdett? Why does Dude help him? We feel we know the answers to all these questions, though they are never spelt out. All are essential to the film, and to what Hawks stands for.

The flooring of Chance establishes the basis on which Dude's whole development is built—his reluctance to be dragged up from his gutter when it is so much easier to sink further; and the resentment of the fallen man for the apparently infallible. Chance's single-handed attempt at arresting Joe Burdett in a saloon full of Joe's friends gives us a perfect image of the Hawks hero. There is no element of showing-off nor of self-willed martyrdom: Chance's attitude is rooted in a personal need for self-respect, which demands that an action that must be done be done unquestioningly, without fuss, and alone, even in the teeth of hopeless odds. Dude's intervention sets the pattern for the whole film, where at every crisis Chance is saved by assistance he hasn't asked for or has rejected; but its motivation is equally fundamental to the spirit of

Rio Bravo: Colorado and Chance

the film. When Chance prevented Dude from taking the coin from the spittoon, Dude was made conscious of his degradation; his beating-up by Joe intensifies this consciousness. Above all, he is confronted by two opposite examples: the moral disintegration of Joe, the moral integrity of Chance. On his choice between them depends his salvation as a human being: his decision to help Chance (physically) commits him to an attempt to save himself (morally and spiritually). To express all this purely through simple physical actions is profoundly characteristic of Hawks; so is the immediately established positive trend of the character-development. There is nothing glib or sentimental about Hawks's treatment of his characters, but if he can possibly steer them towards salvation, he does. This spirit of generosity, the most creative human characteristic, vivifies all his best films. Even Tony Camonte, in *Scarface*, obviously an exception to any general rule one could make about Hawks's protagonists, becomes most interesting when self-awareness begins, belatedly, to break on him. It is consistently a moral rather than a psychological interest: the cure is always therapeutic, never psycho-analytical (though what happens to Dunson in *Red River* has certain affinities with the process of psycho-analysis).

If in *Rio Bravo* the traditional Western theme of the defence of civilised values is reduced to little more than a pretext, where, then, does Hawks put the emphasis? On values below the social level, but on which social values, if valid, must necessarily be built: man's innate need for self-respect or self-definition. As a motif, it will be easily seen that this pervades the film, as a unifying principle of composition. It is stated through virtually every character, usually on his first appearance, like the subject of a fugue, and developed throughout contrapuntally with fugal rigour. The film's first actions constitute a negative statement (Dude grovelling for the coin in the spittoon) and a positive one (Chance's intervention, and the ensuing arrest of Joe Burdett). The first words of Colorado (Ricky Nelson) insist on his rights as an individual: when Chance questions Pat Wheeler (Ward

Bond) about him in his presence, he interrupts with, 'I speak English, Sheriff, you wanna ask me.' Pat, too old and unsteady to be of direct use, risking (and giving) his life to get others to help Chance; Stumpy asserting his independence by disobeying Chance's orders and standing in the jail ,doorway; Feathers refusing to stop gambling and wearing feathers as a way of escaping a suspect past ('That's what I'd do if I were the kind of girl that you think I am'); Carlos insisting with sudden touching dignity on his right to arrange matters as he pleases in his own hotel: all these constitute variants on the theme. *Variants*, not repetitions: the statements range from broad humour (Stumpy) to near tragedy (Dude): each is distinct from the others in tone and in moral weight. Examples could be multiplied throughout the film. There is a continual sense of the contrapuntal interaction of the various levels of seriousness and humour, so that great complexity of tone often results. Consider for example the way in which Stumpy's comic need to emphasise his alertness and mastery to offset his sense of disability ('Old cripples ain't wanted') precipitates Dude's breakdown when Stumpy shoots, as ordered, the moment someone fails to give the word on entering the jail (Dude, bathed and shaved, was unrecognisable). Everything in the film can be referred back to this unifying motif, yet, as always, it is nowhere given explicit statement. The density of the thematic development is increased by the element of parody introduced through the villains. Nathan Burdett (John Russell) goes to such lengths to get his brother out of jail not from motives of affection but from pride in his position: his actions are dictated, that is to say, by the desire not to lose face, a caricature of the motives for which the heroes act, rendered further invalid by the fact that he is defending a morally indefensible action. When Nathan tells Dude that everyone should have a taste of power before he dies, we are made strongly aware of the distinction between the kind of power Dude is experiencing in overcoming his tendency to disintegration, and the sort of power Burdett experiences.

By shifting the emphasis from man's responsibility to society (still there as a starting-point but no more than that) to his

responsibility to himself, Hawks strips everything down to a basic stoic principle. From this follows his conception of friendship as a relationship based on mutual respect and mutual independence. Throughout the film we see Chance training Dude for the independence and self-respect that constitutes true manhood— for a relationship based on a balance of equality between free men. There are those who can see no more to this theme of close friendship between men in Hawks's films than the endorsement of a hearty, superficial matiness: nothing could be further from the truth. These relationships in Hawks almost invariably embody something strong, positive, and fruitful: at the least (*The Thing*) a warmth of mutual response; at the most (*Rio Bravo*) the veritable salvation of a human being.

Here, too, the essential things are conveyed through—or more accurately perhaps *grow out of*—physical actions. It is worth quoting Hawks here—a passage from the earlier of the two interviews he gave Peter Bogdanovich which throws much light on his methods:

> '. . . we have to feel our way as we go along and we can add to a character or get a piece of business between two people and start some relationship going and then further it. In *Rio Bravo* Dean Martin had a bit in which he was required to roll a cigarette. His fingers weren't equal to it and Wayne kept passing him cigarettes. All of a sudden you realise that they are awfully good friends or he wouldn't be doing it. That grew out of Martin's asking me one day "Well, if my fingers are shaky, how can I roll this thing?" So Wayne said, "Here, I'll hand you one", and suddenly we had something going. . . .'

There is a beautiful example in *Only Angels Have Wings* of the establishment of a relationship purely through actions: the scene where Cary Grant and Thomas Mitchell try to guide Joe down through the fog. Hawks builds the scene on a sense of instinctive awareness between the two men, Mitchell using his ears and Grant his voice as if they were two aspects of the same human being; at the end, when Joe has crashed, Mitchell holds out a cigarette he has rolled and Grant takes it, as if he knew it would be exactly there at exactly that moment, without looking. One moment in *Rio Bravo*, in itself very small, beautifully defines the relationship between Chance and Dude. Chance takes Dude out to patrol the streets, mainly to help him overcome the strain he is under from his need for alcohol, pauses by the paid gunman who has been appointed by Burdett to watch the jail, says 'Good evening' to him and stands there till the man shuffles uneasily and moves away. We see Dude watching from the other side of the street, and from his face the impact on him of this expression of moral force, the authority that comes from integrity.

But for Hawks there comes a point where these friendships, valuable and creative as they are, reach the limit of their power to influence and affect, beyond which point the individual is alone with his own resources or sheer chance to fall back on. We saw this in the treatment of Kid's death in *Only Angels Have Wings*; in *Rio Bravo* Dude's salvation rests ultimately, not on Chance, but on chance. At the climax of his relapse, when he has failed in his responsibilities and decided to hand in his badge, he clumsily pours out a glass of whisky, nerves gone, hands trembling helplessly: it is his moment of defeat, from which it seems likely that he will never recover. Chance's example, combined with his stoic refusal to indulge him, no longer reaches him. Then, as he raises the glass, the 'Alamo' music starts up again from the saloon across the street, and we see its immediate implications ('No quarter!'—it is being played on Burdett's orders) and its heroic associations strike him. He pauses, then pours the whisky back into the thin-necked bottle unfalteringly—'Didn't spill a drop.' It is his moment of victory, and one of the great moments of the cinema. Its power to move derives partly from its context (it is, after all, one of the central moments in a film single-mindedly concerned with self-respect), partly from the irony (the tune played to undermine courage in fact has the opposite effect), and partly on our sense of the precariousness of everything.

One of the concerns common to *Red River* and *Rio Bravo*— though it takes very different forms in the two films—is a preoccupation with heroism, the conditions necessary to it, and the human limitations that accompany those conditions. This will be obvious enough in the earlier film, with its examination of the limits of the acceptability of Dunson's ruthlessness. The concept of the hero in *Rio Bravo*—of Hawks's attitude to him—may at first sight appear less complex, in that Chance is presented throughout as morally infallible. Yet Hawks's conception here is subtler. Without qualifying our sense of moral infallibility, Hawks defines in the course of the action the limitations that not only accompany it but are to some extent the conditions for its existence. Consider, for example, the song sequence, one of the film's focal points (it is often regarded as an irrelevance, forced into the action to give Ricky Nelson something to sing). It occurs just after Dude's triumph over his weakness, which in its turn was preceded by Colorado's intervention, his ceasing to 'mind his own business', in the flower-pot scene. Earlier, his refusal to commit himself helped to make possible the murder of his boss, Pat Wheeler: Colorado, like Dude, was guilty of a failure of responsibility. In the song sequence he, Dude, and Stumpy sit in a circle in the jail, Stumpy accompanying on the harmonica while the other two sing. It is perhaps the best expression in Hawks's work of the spontaneous-intuitive sympathy which he makes so important as the basis of human relations. The compositions and the editing (by making us aware of the exchange of glances) as well as the acting contribute gradually to link the three men in a bond of fellow-feeling through the shared experience of the music. Throughout it, Chance stands outside the circle looking on, a paternally approving smile on his face, but none the less excluded from the common experience. The three physically or morally fallible men—cripple, reformed drunk, boy who failed once in his responsibility—are able to achieve a communion which the infallible man is denied, excluded by his very infallibility.

More obviously, Chance's limitations are revealed in his relationship with Feathers. For, if *Rio Bravo* as a whole is a summing-up of Hawks's adventure films, its love relationship, with the repeated discomfiture of the hero, succinctly recapitulates

Rio Bravo: Stumpy, Dude and Colorado—the song sequence

Hawksian comedy, and the film is enormously enriched by the interaction of the two. It is the first time in Hawks's work that this kind of relationship, so basic to the comedies, appears in an adventure film. Certainly the Grant/Arthur and Bogart/Bacall relationships in *Only Angels Have Wings* and *To Have and Have Not* have points in common with it; but Grant and Bogart, while they may have *resisted* their women for a time, were always able to handle them. *Rio Bravo* marks the beginning of a tendency (here kept beautifully under control and in balance) to satirise the hero—a tendency carried further with Wayne in *Hatari!*, and taking different forms in the parodistic 'Wildcat Jones' song of *Red Line 7000* and in *El Dorado*, where the challenge comes not from women but from age.

Feathers's first appearance constitutes a humorous inversion of the fugue theme—Chance, the seemingly invulnerable, almost mythic figure of the 'strong, silent man', finding his dignity abruptly undermined when the scarlet bloomers ordered for

Carlos's wife are held up against him for Carlos's approval, and the woman greets him with, 'Those things have great possibilities, Sheriff, but not on you.' She has to take the initiative throughout their relationship; but—and this is what makes it so different from the man-woman relationship in, say, *I Was a Male War Bride*—its development is repeatedly given impetus by her attempts to drive him to establish authority over her, thereby completing his mastery of his world. Feathers, in fact, trains Chance rather as Chance trains Dude—trains him for a relationship of spiritual equals, for it is always clear that the establishment of male authority will be a matter of voluntary surrender on her part. It is true that Hawks never shows his man-woman relationships developing beyond a certain point; nevertheless, the relationship reached at the end of *Rio Bravo* carries a beautiful and satisfying sense of maturity, with both partners strong enough to preserve a certain independence and to come together on terms of equality. Again, it is a relationship of free people, each existing from an established centre of self-respect. The final scene between them, where Chance 'tells her he loves her' by ordering her not to go down to the saloon to sing in the very revealing 'entertainer's' costume which she wore before she knew him, far from seeming an anti-climax after the gun-and-dynamite showdown with Burdett and his men, is the true climax of the film. The lightly humorous treatment shouldn't blind us to its underlying seriousness and beauty.

There is a sense in which Chance's independence and self-sufficiency is illusory. He goes through the film systematically rejecting the help of others; yet every crisis without exception, from the arrest of Joe Burdett on, would end in disaster were it not for the unsolicited intervention of others. Without the cripple, the drunk, the comic Mexican, the teenage boy, a girl on hand to fling a well-timed flower-pot, the superman would be defeated before he had the chance to perform a single decisive action. Yet if the others are physically indispensable to him, it is never in doubt that Chance is spiritually indispensable to them. Remove him from the film, and you would be left largely with human

54

wreckage; for it is abundantly clear that it is Chance, partly by direct influence, partly by example, by the very fact of his existence, who gives meaning, coherence, and integrity to the lives of those around him. As a concrete embodiment of the Hawksian values, he is the nucleus round which the others can organise themselves, without which there would be no possibility of order.

I am aware that this account of *Rio Bravo* is open to one serious objection: anyone reading it, with its talk of fugues, of stylistic and structural rigour, of moral seriousness, will be totally unprepared for the consistently relaxed, delightful, utterly unpretentious film that *Rio Bravo* is. In fact, when it first came out, almost nobody noticed that it was in any sense a serious work of art. Furthermore, it would be a great mistake to assume that there is any split here between the relaxed tone and the serious content —that Hawks has 'something to say', a 'message', and has deliberately (and compromisingly) made it 'entertaining', sugaring the moral pill, so to speak, for the masses. One can feel confident that *Rio Bravo* is precisely the film he wanted to make. The immense good humour is, in fact, essential to the moral tone, and, together with the leisurely tempo, manifests an achieved serenity of mind; the relaxed mood of the film as a whole is never incompatible with the consistent tension in the relationships that shows the intensity of Hawks's involvement in his work.

The source of *Rio Bravo*'s richness is threefold: there is the sense of it as the product of a whole vital tradition, acting as a fruitful soil in which the film is rooted, nourishing it invisibly from beneath; and there is the sense of the film's working on many levels and for different sorts of spectator, the strength derived from its being the product and the representative of a popular art form, appealing to 'groundlings' and intellectuals alike, and with no sense of discrepancy or conflict between these levels of appeal. But above all the richness derives from Hawks himself, from the warmth and generosity of his personality, pervading every scene of the film; from the essentially positive and creative nature of all the film's leading relationships; from the good humour and sanity that colour every sequence. Everything in *Rio Bravo* ends happily;

not a hero dies, the final battle becomes a kind of joyous celebration-party for Dude's regeneration. Yet always one is aware of the extreme precariousness of everything. In the background, never very far away, is the eternal darkness surrounding human existence, against which the Hawksian stoicism shines; over everything, colouring each scene, is the marvellous good-natured humour and balance of Hawks when he is at his best.

3: The Lure of Irresponsibility

Scarface (1932), *Bringing up Baby* (1938), *His Girl Friday* (1940), *Monkey Business* (1952), *I Was a Male War Bride* (1949)

Scarface

It may seem perverse to approach the comedies via a gangster film of exceptional ferocity, almost the only Hawks film in which the protagonist dies. But *Scarface* belongs with the comedies.

There are interesting parallels between *Scarface* and Godard's *Les Carabiniers*. Though utterly different in style and method, both have leading characters who consistently perform monstrous violent actions which the films never condone, yet who retain the audience's sympathy to the end, and for similar reasons. Godard gives his Michelangelo the characteristics, not only of a primitive, but of a young child, an innocent immune from moral judgements because he has never developed moral awareness. Far from weakening the statement of horror and despair, this intensifies it.

Tony Camonte (Paul Muni), the 'hero' of *Scarface*, is always touching and eventually pathetic, because he too is an innocent. Indeed, he captures and keeps more of the spectator's affection than Michelangelo; this is surprising, because Hawks allows us to see him killing sympathetic characters (Guino Rinaldo), where Godard keeps the slaughter in *Les Carabiniers* strictly impersonal; but Hawks's method, though consistently objective, allows us much closer to the characters than Godard's. There is one basic difference between the two films: *Scarface* remains firmly within the conventions of naturalism, whereas *Les Carabiniers* refuses all such limitations (thereby discovering limitations of its own). The difference is apparent in the 'childlike' presentation of Tony and Michelangelo (and even in their names). Tony's primitivism is entirely credible naturalistically, where Michelangelo's infantilism is very stylised.

Tony is introduced as a squat shadow, evoking ape or Neanderthaler. His fascinated attraction to gaudy trappings (loud dressing-gowns, ties, jewellery, etc.) recalls the savage's fondness for beads. His attempts at elegance—large acreage of handkerchief protruding from breast pocket, huge tie—are grotesque. With this goes his ignorance. When Poppy (Karen Morley) tells him that jewellery on men is 'effeminate' he is boyishly delighted, automatically assuming a compliment. When she tells him his place is 'kind of gaudy', his reply is 'Isn't it though? Glad you like it.' When he rises to power as Johnny Lovo's right-hand man, he wears a new shirt each day, sports an even fancier dressing-gown than Lovo's, boasts to Poppy of having several more suits, 'all different colours', jumps up and down on the bed showing it to her, saying, 'It's got inside springs. Bought it at an auction.' His attempts at seduction show a childlike *naïveté* which eventually, touching Poppy, becomes an important factor in her capitulation. His infantile confusion of values—woman and dressing-gown placed on roughly the same level, half gaudy toys, half status symbols—anticipates interestingly Michelangelo's response to the *carabinier's* catalogue of the treasures of the world that he will bring back as loot.

This essential innocence is reflected in other characters. The fat Italian gangster Costillo, celebrating at a New Year's Eve party, paper-hatted amidst a debris of festoons among which is a discarded bra, boasts childishly of his prosperity (he is about to get shot), mentioning in the same breath the girl and the automobile that he can now afford. Guino Rinaldo (George Raft), when Cesca (Ann Dvorak) calls on him, is cutting out paper dolls; and it is he, the tough gangster, who is seduced by the sheltered Cesca. As Tony comes to kill Guino, Cesca is singing a comic song about a train-driver, complete with 'poop-poop' noises. Tony's illiterate secretary has continual difficulty with telephones: he is afraid of them, and at one point wants to shoot one. Both here and in *Les Carabiniers* we are made to feel the frightening discrepancy between the achievements of civilisation and the actual level of culture attained by the individuals who are its by-products.

Characteristically—though, considering the ostensible subject of *Scarface*, remarkably—there is little sense of social context. Members of normal society appear only as the merest background figures (waiters in the machine-gunned restaurant, nurses held up in the hospital where Meehan is finished off). Considered too simply, *Scarface* appears a dangerously immoral film. It opens with an explicitly moralising foreword about '. . . the intention of the producer . . .', and halfway through there is an embarrassingly hammy scene (added by another director, apparently, as a safeguard against censorship) where a newspaper editor accused of sensationalism defends his position, arguing the need to expose outrages. But the film shows remarkably little society either to outrage or to defend. Hawks's 'naturalism' is highly selective: he works by simply eliminating society. Hence in *Scarface* the ostensible subject—society threatened by gangsters—isn't really treated at all. We see almost nothing of the results of the outrages—bomb explosions, machine-gunning—in terms of human suffering. The police are uniformly unsympathetic. Hawks presents his gang wars as kids' games played with real bullets. A sardonic, macabre humour is seldom absent, and some of the outrages are treated as uninhibited farce: Gaffney's machine-gunning of the restaurant, with Tony's secretary struggling to cope with the telephone—an attempt continued, doggedly, throughout the attack, with boiling tea pouring out over his bottom through the bullet-holes in an urn. The film communicates, strongly, a sense of exhilaration: Hawks actually encourages us to share the gangsters' enjoyment of violence. If Tony has the innocence of a child or a savage, he also has the energy and vitality that goes with it.

Yet no one with a sensibility more developed than Tony Camonte's could find *Scarface* ultimately immoral. The attitude to Tony is complex. If we regard him sympathetically, we never feel that he is being glorified. His pitiful end is implicit throughout. He is funny and touching because he is an overgrown child, emotionally arrested at an early stage, with no sympathetic awareness of others and no self-awareness. He dies when he loses his essential innocence —when, in a very shadowy, disturbing way, he begins to see himself, and his armour of boyish self-confidence, like his steel shutters ('I got nobody—I'm all alone—my steel shutters don't work'), is no longer any protection.

How, then, does Hawks 'place' this monstrous innocence and its effects?—why, if the killings are often exhilarating and farcical, are they also so disturbing? Hawks faced a difficult problem: how to discover images or references which could be incorporated unostentatiously within the naturalistic conventions? Instead of inviting judgement on the gangsters for subverting the social order, Hawks disturbs our response to the film's humour with images and leitmotifs, very simple and traditional yet the more evocative because of it, with their accumulated associations. One thinks of the passage from Borges which Godard quotes at the start of *Les Carabiniers*: the writer returns increasingly to the 'old metaphors' because they are enriched by past usage.

The image of the cross pervades the whole film. It is the first thing we see; every killing is accompanied (often unobtrusively) by a cross, sometimes formed by patterns of light or shadow; the scar on Tony's face is a cross. In the scene of the St Valentine's Day Massacre the camera moves down from seven crosses—the pattern in a wooden overhang—to show the seven victims. The majority of these are the multiplication-sign form of the cross—a straightforward sign for death, the crossing-out of a human being; but several take the traditional Christian shape. The pervasive image carries associative emotional overtones which contribute importantly to the effect of the killings. Individual instances carry their own overtones. Near the end of the film Tony, incestuously involved with Cesca without understanding the nature of his own feelings, kills Guino out of possessive jealousy; at the first meeting of Guino and Cesca, Guino is seen through a cross formed by the balcony edge and its support. The effect is very unobtrusive— Hawks never sacrifices the action of a scene to symbolism—but we are by that time sufficiently used to the association of the crosses with killings for it to carry an emotional charge. Lighting is of great importance in *Scarface*: in the scene where Gaffney (Boris Karloff) is shown the concrete results of the St Valentine's Day Massacre, and he, among the most ruthless of the film's killers, is morally outraged, the accompanying cross is a radiant white. At another point the cross—Christian shape—is part of an undertaker's sign, shot from above so that it hangs over the body like a cross at a funeral. The associations give the killings a particular flavour of profanity.

For many of the killings in *Scarface* Hawks finds vivid epitomising images. In the bowling alley Gaffney rolls a ball, the sound of gunfire tells us he has been killed, and then as the shot continues we watch the progress of the bowling ball until it knocks over all the ninepins. Gaffney will never know his throw was so successful. More than any face-contorting and stomach-clutching, the shot conveys the finality of death, in a manner no less moving for being detached and indirect. Later, when Tony shoots Guino for touching Cesca (they are in fact married), Guino dies while the coin he has flipped is still in the air: its falling to the ground, after all the previous occasions on which he has infallibly caught it, conveys the fact of his death with great intensity. The death of Tony's secretary makes similar use of habitual behaviour: he dies, mortally wounded by bullets through the door he has just closed, struggling to cope with the telephone that has defeated him throughout the film. But all the comic quality has gone, removed with the ill-fitting hat he automatically takes off as he staggers back from the door: his illiteracy, his unquestioning devotion to Tony, his funny clothes, his total childlike inadequacy in coping with his environment, are no longer in the least funny, and we are left with a sense of terrible waste.

Other images and references in *Scarface* associate with the crosses. One in the historical data—the traditional associations of St Valentine's Day giving the massacre an extra profanity—is neatly underlined by the killers' brutal talk about 'bringing you a valentine'. Earlier, Gaffney's attack on the restaurant was made under cover of a funeral procession, the machine-gun hidden in

62

the hearse. In two scenes flowers are used. Tony's men enter a hospital to finish off Meehan, survivor—though badly injured—of a previous attack. The intensity and terrible poetry of the scene are partly the product of its economy: no preliminaries, simply a brief sequence of shots of the gangsters, carrying bouquets, holding up terrified nurses in a corridor, opening a door beyond which is a heavily bandaged figure in a bed, with one leg strapped up, unable to move to cover, the leg support casting a cross-shaped shadow on the far wall. The figure is blasted with bullets, then a bouquet is flung in on the body as a parting cynicism. The scene (it is all over in a few seconds) epitomises the disturbing power of the film. The tension and pace of direction and editing capture a sense of exhilaration, we respond to the uninhibited audacity of the gangsters, their freedom from all social and moral restraints, their ability to perform outrageous actions in the face of social institutions. At the same time the horror of the scene is over-whelming: only a Tony in the audience could find it *merely* exhilarating. As elsewhere in Hawks's work (*Monkey Business* offering the extremest instance), our yearnings for total irresponsibility are evoked to be chastised. Through the images of cross and flowers, the utter helplessness of the victim, the values appealed to are absolute rather than social; our horror derives from deeper sources than the violation of social stability.

The other scene centred on a flower is equally complex and disturbing. Guino Rinaldo brings Tony a rose as a token that he has killed a rival who ran a flower-shop. Tony later in the scene gives it to Poppy, whom he is trying to seduce. The scene evokes the rose's traditional associations with love and beauty, tenderness and transience, and juxtaposes these with our knowledge of its actual *dramatic* significance.

Hawks, like Godard, uses the arts to suggest more developed values beyond the reach of the characters; though the examples in Hawks's film are again much simpler, and entirely integrated in the action. Tony's signature tune, whistled every time he kills (the sextet from Donizetti's *Lucia di Lammermoor*, 'Chi me frena?', What restrains me?) gives his first appearance an almost surrealist quality: the squat ape-like shadow juxtaposed with the elegant phrases of Italian opera. His visit to the theatre and his reactions to the play (*Rain*) anticipate *Les Carabiniers'* cinema scene. Tony does not, like Michelangelo, totally misunderstand the nature of the medium; but his attitude shows a similarly elementary contact. His dimly awakening sense of the existence of moral problems foreshadows his downfall: he is quite unable to grasp their nature, let alone cope with them. He tries to explain the play to his secretary, who prefers 'shows with jokes': 'This Sadie, she's a girl with a problem. . . . She's what you call disillusioned.' He leaves the secretary to find out how the play ends while he goes to another killing that can't wait, and when he gets the garbled report, gives Sadie's solution (she 'climbed back in the hay with the army') his delighted approval. His incomprehension of the issues (counterpointed with his further progress in bloodshed) beautifully defines the terrible innocence that permits him to kill and plunder, and which also allows him not to question his attachment to Cesca or his immediate ferocious jealousy of any man who comes near her.

In the scenes of Tony's muddled self-realisation and subsequent death the film's moral force becomes finally evident. Far from being a 'moral' ending hastily tacked on in an attempt to make an immoral film respectable, it is as inevitable as the ending of *A Bout de Souffle*. Tony is strong only while he remains unaware. The shooting of Guino and Cesca's ensuing outcry are crucial. Tony loses control over her because he is losing control over himself— we see from his facial expression, from his inability, now, to hold her, his dim, reluctant realisation of what his real feelings for her are. When Tony's secretary dies struggling with the phone, it is Poppy on the other end. All Tony can find to say to her is a vague, confused, 'I didn't know', which can refer simply to the dead secretary—Tony hadn't realised that he was hit—or to the realisation of his own involvement with Cesca (which makes Poppy no longer of the slightest importance to him). The ambiguity prevents us from applying the words narrowly: they sum up Tony's whole appalling ignorance: after all the massacres, the audacities, the

Scarface: Tony and Cesca

exhilaration, the success, they are all he can find to say for himself. After it, his reaction to Cesca's failure to kill him is 'Why didn't you shoot?'—followed by a hysterical defiance of the encircling police which grotesquely parodies the exhilaration of the violence earlier in the film. His hysterical triumphant laughter coincides with Cesca's being struck by a bullet—which ricochets off the much-vaunted steel shutter, symbol to Tony of his invulnerability, which he is holding open at that moment. The cross that has accompanied all Tony's killings is appropriately, though ironically, there for the death of his sister; after which his disintegration into blind panic as the gas bombs explode around him—the rising and overpowering clouds of gas providing the perfect visual expression for his bewildered state of mind, the protective innocence punctured—stands as judgement on all his past.

The essential condemnation of Tony Camonte, like that of Michel Poiccard in *A Bout de Souffle*, whose anti-social behaviour also conveys to the audience an irresistible exhilaration, is not imposed from any external moral standpoint (despite *Scarface*'s foreword to the effect that '. . . Justice always catches up with the criminal who must answer for his sins'), but is arrived at empirically in terms of the character's own development. Tony and Michel condemn themselves, ultimately, because their behaviour is self-destructive, not only in the simple, literal sense that it gets them killed, but because it denies them fulfilment of their basic needs. Both directors have the courage to treat their characters' rejection of responsibility and rush towards self-destruction inwardly, with the implicit admission that they are dealing with universal traits and urges. A dangerous method (both films have been accused of immorality); but valid morality must be based on honesty.

The comparison with Godard reveals Hawks's strength and limitations. At first sight *Scarface* seems richer than *Les Carabiniers*. It works brilliantly on a popular narrative level, a dimension that Godard's film doesn't pretend to. Beyond this is the essential stability of Hawks's character and the traditional nature of his art: his successful films are pervaded by a robustness derived from stable values—loyalty, courage, endurance, mastery of self and environment—whereas the emotion underlying and characterising *Les Carabiniers* is a terrible despair, arising from Godard's exposure to the complexities and confusions, the disintegration of accepted values, inherent in contemporary society. *Les Carabiniers* is a statement about the modern world of a kind Hawks nowhere attempts. This defines him as an artist—it doesn't invalidate him. Hawks takes the state of civilisation for granted in a way that has become increasingly difficult for the modern artist, and he has been helped in this by the availability to him of cinematic traditions which manifest themselves in the genres, but his inability to make statements about modern society limits his work, affecting particularly certain of the comedies.

It is with the comedies that *Scarface* unquestionably belongs. It has almost nothing in common with the adventure films (besides the enclosed group); it has almost everything in common with the comedies. The overlapping and combining of farce and horror points ahead to *His Girl Friday*, Tony's destructive innocence to that of Lorelei Lee; in *Monkey Business*, the juxtapositions of ape, savages, and children are clearly related to the presentation of the gangsters in *Scarface*. Above all, *Scarface* gives us the essential theme of Hawks's most characteristic comedies. If the adventure films place high value on the sense of responsibility, the comedies derive much of their tension and intensity from the fascination exerted by irresponsibility. I pass now to two films in which this fascination is not quite under control.

Bringing up Baby

Bringing up Baby is perhaps the funniest of Hawks's comedies but not the best. Again and again, after no matter how many viewings, the spectator is delighted by small touches of comic business often beyond the critic's reach, since they defy verbal description: matters of gesture, expression, intonation. Consider the little scene where the delivery-man brings Professor David Huxley (Cary Grant) the intercostal clavicle while David is speaking on the telephone to his fiancée: one or two laconic comments by the delivery-man ('Don't let it throw you, buster') aside, the humour lies in the way the characters are standing, the way they look at each other, the way they speak. Or there is the moment when David, in an elaborately feminine negligée, opens the front door to Katherine Hepburn's aunt, a determined masculine-looking woman in manly tweeds, and, already driven to near-frenzy by the systematic humiliations to which he has been subjected, in answer to her question as to what he's doing dressed like *that*, gives a frenetic little leap in the air, waggles his arms, and shouts 'I went gay suddenly.' It is a moment that epitomises many of the essentials of Hawksian comedy. There is the extremeness of it, in the context of the light comedy genre: we are almost in the world of the Marx Brothers. There is the sexual reversal, the humiliation of the male, his loss of mastery, which makes the comedies an inversion of the adventure films. Finally, there is the *resilience* of the male, his ability to live through extremes of humiliation retaining an innate dignity.

Bringing Up Baby: David and Susan

The inspiration isn't consistent. The tension throughout is in the Grant-Hepburn relationship; scenes involving minor characters are sometimes laboured. Major Horace Applegate (Charles Ruggles), the effeminate and ineffectual big-game hunter, is interesting as a crazy-mirror reflection of the men of action, dominant and professional, who people the adventure films, but somewhat tedious in himself. Barry Fitzgerald's drunken Irish gardener seems predictable. Worse, the invention flags in the middle of the film, even in scenes involving the principals. During the first hour, with Hepburn ruining Grant's golf-game with an important business connection, bringing every conceivable disaster upon him in a night-club, then blackmailing him into helping her take Baby (her leopard) to Connecticut, the inspiration, both in script and direction, never lets up. But later, in the scenes where the two search for the missing leopard in the woods at night, conception and execution falter, the material is thin and directional inspiration more spasmodic. Incidents where characters fall down banks and get entangled in poison ivy are not very funny, nor do they add much in terms of thematic development. With the release of the dangerous circus leopard the film picks up again and the invention regains something of its previous density; but the sense of *élan*, once lost, is hard to recapture.

The real nature of the flaw in *Bringing up Baby* lies deeper, and is far more revealing of Hawks's limitations and weaknesses. The structure is satisfyingly bold and symmetrical, with leanings towards allegory, built on oppositions. In the centre is Professor Huxley, on the surface entirely dedicated to zoological research (the reconstruction of a dinosaur skeleton). On one side is his mousy, earnest, sexless secretary-fiancée, who refuses a honeymoon on the grounds that it would interfere with his work; on the other there is Susan (Hepburn). It is easy to see them as Duty (conceived as deadeningly dry and repressive) and Nature (conceived as amoral and entirely irresponsible); and tempting to simplify further (the film encourages it) and see them in Freudian terms as Superego and Id. David's dedication to his work *isn't* complete: in his extreme absent-mindedness, his inability to cope practically with situations, we feel inner forces working against it; and we note that *he* wants a honeymoon even if his bride-to-be doesn't. Hepburn erupts at moments when he is about to clinch a deal that will ensure his future; and each time she shatters to fragments the superficial order of his life. Once she has materialised, he is completely helpless against her. The entire characterisation of Susan favours this interpretation. She is not so much *im*moral as *a*moral: she seems never to feel a twinge of guilt, never acknowledging responsibility for the comic disasters she precipitates. The opposition of the two women in the film's basic pattern is reinforced by the equally clear-cut opposition of animals, living and dead: the dinosaur skeleton (represented for us during most of the film by the intercostal clavicle) and the leopard, extensions, respectively of David's way of life and Susan's. There is a fairly systematic progression in the film, from the world of the dominance of the Superego to that of the Id: starting amid the most civilised settings—museum, golf-course, night-club—the film moves to the country-house of Susan's aunt, thence to the garden, thence to the woods; and there is a corresponding movement from light to darkness. We pass from the unnatural order of the museum to the natural disorder of the woods at night. One can see a parallel progression in the animals, dead dinosaur, pet terrier, tame leopard, wild leopard, though they are not introduced in quite that order (no one who sees the film will find it as crudely schematic as I have made it sound). The release of the semi-wild leopard, suggesting forces beyond anything Susan represents (even she is terrified of it, when she realises it isn't Baby), clinches this sense of a descent into a dangerous, disordered world of nature.

The Grant and Hepburn characters exist on different levels of reality. The trouble is that they are also a man and a woman, and some of the slackening of tension in the scenes in the woods can be accounted for by the feeling that on this level Hawks simply didn't know what to do with them. This discrepancy between levels gives rise to doubts about the film's resolution, and the total outlook it expresses. With Hepburn as Id-figure the end works rather well. Grant, restored to order, is putting the finishing touches to his life-work, the dinosaur skeleton, at the top of a huge scaffolding. Hepburn reappears and climbs up to him; Grant admits that he has enjoyed their misadventures; and within minutes the entire skeletal structure has collapsed. The dry bones represent his life-work and are an image of his way of life, destroyed finally by the eruption of the Id. But it is impossible to see the film *only* like that: one is forced also to contemplate Hepburn as a suitable life-partner for him. One can only feel uneasy, and question whether the triumph of total irresponsibility the film appears to be offering as fitting resolution is in fact acceptable. There is no sense of a possible synthesis or even compromise; the only alternative to Susan is made so ridiculous as to be instantly discounted. Hasn't the temptation to irresponsibility, that gives *Scarface* and *Monkey Business* their tension and vividness, here got the better of Hawks's judgement?—as it is to do again, and more disturbingly, in *His Girl Friday*. And isn't the film's facile ridicule of the stock figure of the Freudian psychiatrist rather revealing?

His Girl Friday

'I was going to prove to somebody one night that *The Front Page* had the finest modern dialogue that had been written, and I asked a girl to read Hildy's part and I read the editor and I stopped and I said, "Hell, it's better between a girl and a man than between two men," and I called Ben Hecht and I said, "What would you think of changing it so that Hildy is a girl?" And he said, "I think it's a great idea," and he came out and we did it.' (Hawks, interviewed by Peter Bogdanovich.)

Consequently, the part of Hildy Johnson, ace reporter for the *Morning Post* whose brilliance makes him indispensable to his editor, played by Pat O'Brien in Lewis Milestone's *The Front Page*, was played by Rosalind Russell in *His Girl Friday*: Hildebrand became Hildegard, his fiancée a fiancé. The decision transforms the whole character of the film, in more ways than may at first be obvious.

Even ignoring the difference in sex, Rosalind Russell's performance is immensely superior to Pat O'Brien's. In *The Front Page* Hildy's indispensability has to be taken on trust: nothing convinces one of it as a tangible reality. Rosalind Russell conveys an intelligence, quickness, efficiency, and insight that make Walter's need of her, and her fellow journalists' admiration, entirely convincing. But the fact that she is female adds other levels. Hildy in *His Girl Friday* is indispensable to Walter in ways the male partnership of *The Front Page* precluded: she has been married to him and has divorced him: he wants her back in other capacities than that of star reporter.

The Front Page has two centres of interest: (1) Will Walter Burns succeed in preventing Hildy from marrying his fiancée and forsaking the *Morning Post* (and journalism)? (2) Will Earl Williams, pathetic condemned murderer and victim of corrupt local politicians, be hanged? The attempt at balancing the two is undermined by the intrinsic disproportion of significance. No particular values are invested in Hildy beyond mere professional efficiency (and even that not dramatically realised); his fiancée is commonplace, and we are clearly meant to want the engagement broken, but the outcome seems of negligible importance. To ask us, at the end, to focus on so trivial an issue after much more disturbing feelings have been aroused by the Earl Williams plot seems callous. The film's chief virtue—its brilliant dialogue—becomes almost a vice: its dazzle masks an essential heartlessness which the film seems at times to be judging but which is never, in fact, adequately 'placed'. Hawks succeeds in modifying this inherent weakness without removing it: *His Girl Friday*, while it easily eclipses its original, remains a flawed film, though the nature of the flaw becomes somewhat different.

The attempt at balancing the two issues has been abandoned: the first twenty minutes of *His Girl Friday* leaves us in no doubt where the focus of our interest is to be. *The Front Page* begins with prison officials testing the gallows; *His Girl Friday* opens in the offices of the *Morning Post* and the first twenty minutes—which, apart from some snatches of transposed dialogue, have no equivalent in the earlier film—are concerned exclusively with the relationship between Hildy and Walter, the Earl Williams hanging existing (at this stage) purely as a counter in Walter's moves. The Earl Williams plot is kept secondary throughout the film and though we are not left with quite the same sense of cynical triviality at the conclusion, a marriage relationship being in question, we are, I think, still left with considerable uneasiness and dissatisfaction.

To pass from *The Front Page* to *His Girl Friday* is to be made aware all over again of Hawks's genius. His creative collaboration with his actors goes far beyond the efficient professionalism of Milestone. Many small touches of comic invention through gesture and expression give the film its surface aliveness. Two tiny examples to represent this: (1) Grant learns that Hildy is getting married tomorrow; one watches the determination to prevent this form on his face like a reflex as tentative strategies flit across his mind—he rubs his hand, touches the phone, then his hand, as if instinctively, picks up a carnation from the vase on his desk and slips it in his buttonhole. (2) Much later in the film, Grant lavishes on Bensiger a place on his newspaper and a huge salary (neither of which Bensiger will in fact ever get) in order to distract him from opening his roll-top desk (in which the escaped Earl Williams is hidden). Prim, fussy little Bensiger, suddenly and for the first time carried away, slaps him on the back then, realising what he is doing, timidly retracts his hand, shocked at himself.

The humanisation of the whole film is ultimately traceable to the initial decision to make Hildy a woman, but it is *realised* through the direction of the actors. I want first to consider the differences arising from the change of Hildy's sex. The first seems surprising, until we remember that this is a Hawks picture: Hildy, appears far more dominating, confident, and self-reliant ('I can handle him', she tells her fiancé of Walter) than her male counterpart in *The Front Page*. But Hawks's women, independent, even aggressive, as they may be, are always intensely feminine (even Ann Sheridan in *I Was a Male War Bride!*) and Hildy's femininity counts for a great deal. It makes the reporters' admiration for her immediately comprehensible. Hawks gets it, beautifully, both ways: she is twice the man Pat O'Brien was (ready, if necessary, to rugger-tackle a witness to official incompetence—an incident, done with terrific panache, which is not in *The Front Page*), yet she never ceases to be very much a woman. Her femininity makes her desire to 'be respectable, lead a halfway normal life', to 'have babies and take care of them and give them cod liver oil' intrinsically more important. It also adds a new dimension to the camaraderie in the press-room.

The scene with Earl Williams in the death-cell (no equivalent in *The Front Page*) is beautifully judged. Behind it is the highly equivocal 'mission' of the *Morning Post*: to get Earl Williams reprieved on the grounds of insanity (the plea is justifiable—Williams is merely a pawn in a political game—yet Walter Burns is going to exploit it to make journalistic capital). Hildy fastens on the one point Earl remembers from listening to soap-box orators—'Production for use: everything should be made use of'—and prompts him with it to support the insanity plea: what was he

His Girl Friday: Mollie Malloy upbraids the journalists

thinking of when he shot the policeman?—the gun was in his hand
—'production for use'? The morality is dubious, and Hawks keeps
us aware of this by slightly emphasising the pressure Hildy puts on
Earl. At the same time Hildy is but translating into journalese
what is obviously true—Williams is, if not insane, at least unbalanced. Clouding the issue further is Hildy's sympathy for
Williams: the scene is beautifully realised as a meeting between
two people, and what is most important in it cannot be conveyed
by quoting the script. Its most important moment is the line
'Good-bye, Earl; good luck,' as Hildy leaves. The camera is at a
distance from the two characters. We see Earl hunched in his
wretched cage, Hildy leaving to freedom; the essence of the moment
is the precise attitudes in which they are seen, and the completely
unsentimental, yet gentle and sympathetic, way in which Rosalind
Russell delivers the commonplace line.

The importance of another woman's presence when Mollie
Malloy upbraids the journalists for callousness should also be

His Girl Friday: Walter Burns (Cary Grant), Bruce Baldwin and Hildy Johnson

obvious. Hawks gives more weight to this scene than Milestone: the men are more affected by Mollie, their card-game broken up, and one feels that this is due in part to the other woman's presence. Hildy's condemnatory 'Gentlemen of the Press!' as she surveys them from the doorway, really makes itself felt.

His Girl Friday's peculiarly sharp flavour derives from its disturbing complexity of tone, felt even in the relatively unclouded comedy of the opening. Bruce Baldwin (Ralph Bellamy), Hildy's fiancé, is (unlike his opposite number in *The Front Page*) a beautifully created character who, at this stage of the film, is not ridiculous. He represents a life of unadventurous respectability, certainly, but Hawks encourages the actor to build up a characterisation at times almost touching. His innocent reactions to Walter Burns, for whom he discovers an immediate liking, show generosity as much as stupidity, and his treatment of Hildy is gentle and considerate. Our reaction when Walter sets out deliberately to make him ridiculous is therefore not unquestioning approval: our laughter already contains elements of discomfort. In the central passages this complexity becomes far more pronounced: we move abruptly from the very funny, fast, cut-and-thrust dialogue of the journalists to Mollie Malloy's attempted suicide (which Hawks makes more abrupt, hence more devastating, than Milestone), then as quickly into the broad farce of Mrs Baldwin's kidnapping by Diamond Louie. As we laugh at the exchanges between Grant and Russell, and the complications arising from the incursions of Bruce's mother, the Sheriff, the Mayor, we cannot forget that Earl Williams is suffocating inside the roll-top desk, never out of camera-range for long. Our feelings about Earl and Mollie work against our response to the slick, cynical brilliance of Walter Burns, making us question our readiness to laugh at it. By the end, Walter's ethos is thoroughly undermined, as Hawks and the scriptwriters drive him to excess after excess ('I don't care if there's a million dead,' he yells into a phone when, while ordering the front page of his paper clear, he is reminded of the Chinese earthquake). Unfortunately, the film is unable to follow through the implications of this: the implicit judgement on Walter Burns and all he stands for is never allowed much force, and the personal relationship is resolved rather easily in the man's typically inexplicit admission that he loves the woman. We cannot feel (as the film evidently wishes us to) that Hildy has made a satisfactory choice: the life Walter offers her strikes us as at least as constricting as the respectability offered by Bruce.

The flaw in *His Girl Friday* resembles that in *Bringing up Baby*: the choice offered Hildy is much too narrow to be acceptable, the surrender to irresponsibility too easily made, the alternative too glibly rendered ridiculous (given the alternatives the film offers, the only morally acceptable ending would be to have Hildy walk out on *both* men; or to present her capitulation to Walter as tragic). Surrender to irresponsibility seems to be a constant temptation for Hawks: it offers, in the comedies, an escape from the constricting routines of modern society which parallels the more valid escape offered by group societies in the adventure films. This temptation gives the comedies their peculiar intensity. When it is adequately countered by opposition or control, the result can be a masterpiece like *Scarface* or *Monkey Business*; at other times, as in *Bringing up Baby* and *His Girl Friday*, it creates a serious imbalance. Hawks's comedies disturb and disconcert; but we must differentiate clearly between the disturbance that results from a fully realised, fully organised work of art, and the uneasiness produced by unresolved or unbalanced elements in a flawed work.

Monkey Business

Scarface apart, Hawks's greatest comedy is *Monkey Business*. Here the disturbing elements that characterise the comedies are assimilated into an entirely coherent, perfectly proportioned whole.

Like *Bringing up Baby*, *Monkey Business* begins with an absent-minded Cary Grant (this time Professor Barnaby Fulton); but here the background to the absent-mindedness is not a skeletal dinosaur and an equally arid fiancée, but an apparently successful and stable marriage. Edwina (Ginger Rogers) is indeed remarkably patient and sympathetic. They are going to a party; after a few unsuccessful attempts to get her husband to carry out some very simple instructions about putting on and off appropriate lights and closing a door with himself on the *outside*, she gives up and they settle down to work on his preoccupation. It takes him some time even to realise that they haven't gone out. Briefly they discuss their marriage (and will do so again in the film's central—in all ways—scene): their lives have become something of a routine. The routine has been broken tonight, certainly, by staying away from a party; but they have stayed home for intellectual reasons; they recall another party they once stayed home from for non-intellectual reasons, with regret that that doesn't happen any more. We also notice that Edwina treats Barnaby as if he were a young and slightly retarded child. Soon Hank Entwhistle (Hugh Marlowe) arrives, an old flame of Edwina's, now a friend-of-the-family. The three have a very civilised relationship, with no apparent tensions; though there is a certain amount of playful harping on whether Edwina shouldn't have married Hank. If on the whole we still

Monkey Business: Edwina, Barnaby and Mr Oxly

have the impression of a happy, stable marriage, we have come to feel, I think, that the happiness and stability depend on the *suppression* of quite a lot that is never mentioned and scarcely thought about. No one would guess the development of *Monkey Business* from this opening; but the seeds have all been planted.

Barnaby's preoccupation is a drug, tentatively christened B-4 (they can advertise it as 'B-4 and after'), which he is supposed to be discovering: a drug to restore people's youth. Barnaby can't get the ingredients right. Unknown to anyone, the drug is mixed correctly and poured into the laboratory drinking water supply by an escaped chimpanzee; the main part of *Monkey Business* starts from this premise. In the first half of the film Barnaby and Edwina drink the water in turn and revert to teenagers; in the second half they drink an overdose simultaneously and revert to young children (in all cases without *physical* change beyond such things as improved vision and cured back-aches).

They do not revert to the teenagers they once were. We are told nothing about Barnaby's youth, but we do not believe, from the adult we have seen, that he ever had crew-cuts, drove sports cars recklessly over town, wore far-out socks, ties, jackets. We *are* told that in her teens Edwina was a serious and dedicated student of ichthyology: we cannot imagine her as either the wildly undisciplined and demanding teenager or the shy, shrinking virgin that she alternates between under the influence of the drug. 'B-4' releases all the things they *weren't*. There is a splendid moment when Barnaby (buying his sports car) sees the legs of his boss's secretary Miss Laurel (Marilyn Monroe) walking past under a billboard and recognises their owner from them unhesitatingly. It is so funny in itself that we may miss the essential point: earlier in the film she asked him to examine her stockings, and the joke then derived from his seeing *only* the stockings, not what was inside them. He has registered the legs subconsciously only; and it is the subconscious that B-4 releases. What Barnaby records (with reference both to his own and Edwina's behaviour under the influence of the drug) is 'Complete reversal of normal behaviour pattern.'

The comedy of the first half of *Monkey Business* is so fast and funny that we scarcely have time to realise what is happening. The second reversion over, Barnaby and Edwina go to the laboratory to record reactions—and perhaps to destroy the formula (the mixture they *think* has affected them, in fact perfectly innocuous). It is difficult to see what more can happen. Both are subdued and restless: we sense things unspoken between them. Then they—and we—begin to grasp the full implications of their behaviour. Barnaby has flirted with, and been kissed by, Miss Laurel; Edwina has demanded a divorce from her 'cruel' husband and contacted Hank Entwhistle; both have cast off all inhibitions, all sense of decorum and responsibility. Barnaby confronts Edwina with the facts; she hedges, saying, 'It was just the formula.' To which Barnaby retorts, 'Oh, I understand it was the formula that brought it out. . . .' He talks of 'subconscious aversion', 'buried resentments'; they are brought to admit that they are 'having doubts' about their marriage. In fact, more even than their marriage is in question:

Monkey Business: Barnaby, Edwina and Miss Laurel

the whole basis of their lives. The drug has released all those impulses on the suppression of which their past, and their present and future, stability depend. *Monkey Business* is at once Hawks's most *consistently* funny film, and the one in which he moves closest to tragedy.

Having reached the brink, Barnaby and Edwina move hastily back: he determines to destroy the formula—its implications are too subversive and disturbing, it undermines the whole of civilised existence. At that very moment Edwina turns on the laboratory tap for water for coffee, and Barnaby, slightly on edge, points out that it's not drinking water and directs her to the water in the cooler, in which the *effective* drug is mixed. A moment, for the audience, of extreme panic: a world of subversion and disruption opens up before us: what further can the drug reveal about the Fultons' lives—about *our* lives?

The panic is fully justified by the sequel. One is not surprised at the widespread complaints that the last part of *Monkey Business* goes too far and ceases to be funny; but for those stable enough to accept them the excesses to which Hawks—with ruthless logic—pushes things are the most brilliant part of the film. The reversion to childhood has the effect of removing finally all restraints, all responsibility. Barnaby and Edwina can now do all the things they really wanted to do as adults. The 'subconscious aversions' and 'buried resentments' come out in the scene where they slosh paint over each other with increasing ferocity. Previously, faced with the presence of lipstick on Barnaby's face after his drive with Miss Laurel, Edwina has responded with a charming, sophisticated irony behind which one sensed suppressed jealousy; now she catapults Miss Laurel's backside and tries to assault her. Barnaby, learning that Hank is coming to the house, gets a gang of boys dressed as redskins to lure him to a pole, tie him to it, and half scalp him.

At the end of the film order is restored, but not before all Barnaby's colleagues have drunk overdoses of B-4 and swung around the laboratory with the chimpanzee, squirting each other with soda-water. Man reverts, in the course of the film, not merely to childhood but right back to the ape stage, via the intermediate stage of savagery (the redskins). We have already met the collocation of infant, savage, and ape in the gangsters of *Scarface*; the rather similar principle behind two very different films should now be clear. Both insist on the savagery that underlies civilised life. In discussing *Only Angels Have Wings* I drew attention to the parallels that can be drawn between Hawks and Conrad, and used *Monkey Business* and *Heart of Darkness* to stress the great gulf that divides them. It is true, of course, that Hawks has no equivalent to show for one of the most terrible works in fiction; yet *thematically* (or, if you prefer, in terms of fundamental assumptions about life) the parallel strikingly holds.

The final resolution is simple and beautiful. The water containing the drug has been removed before anyone realised what was in it; the professors are trying to encourage the monkey to repeat its fortuitous success. Meanwhile, Barnaby and Edwina stay home from a night out for non-intellectual reasons. There is no pretence that anything has been solved—what solution could there be to such an analysis of the predicament of civilised man?—but the two face their lives in a spirit of acceptance. Barnaby seems rather more purposeful and in control of things, Edwina less maternal: perhaps she has learnt something from her readiness earlier to accept a nine-month-old baby as her husband, on purely circumstantial evidence?

The reversions in *Monkey Business*, like the anti-social behaviour of the gangsters of *Scarface*, strike sympathetic chords in all of us; the unflagging zest of the film suggests that they strike sympathetic chords in Hawks. This disturbing ambivalence of feeling—the simultaneous attraction to the rational and the instinctive, the civilised and the primitive—is central to much of Hawks's work. We never reach anything remotely approaching 'the horror—the horror' of *Heart of Darkness*; if the descent into primitiveness of *Monkey Business* conveys a sense of dangerous uncontrol it conveys simultaneously a joyous exhilaration. Our primitive selves respond, our civilised selves tell us to be ashamed of the response: this is the tension that underlies *Monkey Business*, and Hawks here keeps the conflicting impulses perfectly in balance, without sacrifice of vitality.

If *Monkey Business* is the greatest of Hawks's comedies, it is finally because it is the most organic. Once the principle has been grasped, every detail of the film fits into place. Barnaby's boss Mr Oxly (Charles Coburn), contemplating with unqualified admiration the imbecilic cavortings of a supposedly rejuvenated chimpanzee suggests, near the beginning of the film, the folly of human desires and reminds us of the connection between the childish and the senile. The 'half-infant' Monroe character stands as an example of fully developed immaturity. Edwina's mother adds a further complexity by showing us that Edwina's early behaviour under the drug—her reversion to helpless, trembling virginity—is just what the mother likes to see, conforming to her image of what a girl should be. Edwina's very first action after taking the drug—the dropping of a fish down Oxly's trousers—with its ironic appropriateness to the dedicated student of ichthyology and its combining of an irresponsible teenage joke with inescapable sexual overtones, shows us very economically the discrepancy between what she was and what the drug allows her to become. Her later assumption that the naked infant that has strayed into the house is her drastically retrogressed husband is anticipated not only in her motherly handling of Barnaby at the beginning, but by her half-gleeful talk about the possibility of his reverting to infancy in the coffee-making scene half-way through. The image of the eminently civilised and scholarly Barnaby daubed with war-paint and executing a war-dance with a gang of kids round a bound and petrified Hank, at whom he brandishes a lethal-looking pair of scissors, crystallises (with its simultaneous sense of the loss of control and the gaining of vitality) the ambivalent feeling of the whole film. There are no irrelevances: the comic invention is the funnier for being so satisfyingly organic.

I Was a Male War Bride

I Was a Male War Bride (released in Great Britain as *You Can't Sleep Here*, but there seems to be general agreement now to call it by its right name) stands apart from the other comedies. Besides being thematically independent, it lacks the organic construction of *Monkey Business* or *Bringing up Baby*. Its general movement is consistent enough: we follow Captain Henri Rochard (Free French army, occupying Germany just after the Second World War)—Cary Grant again—through progressive humiliations, in the first half at the hands of a woman, in the second imposed by officialdom, until the logical culmination has him disguised as a WAAC called Florence, in a wig made from a horse's tail. This general movement is realised in episodes loosely strung together.

That this is the least funny of Hawks's successful comedies, however (for it *is* on the whole successful), lies in its very nature. No other comedy, surely, has looked so drab. The credit sequence, with Grant riding in a jeep past acres of bomb ruins, sets the tone. The settings—military offices, bare corridors, dark inn-room—are uniformly dingy, the lighting even more subdued than usual in a Hawks comedy; there are many night scenes. Even when the film moves briefly out into open country there is no brilliance. The women are in uniform throughout. An oppressive dinginess hangs over the whole film, even in the sequences of most extreme comedy. It noticeably slows down the tempo—there is little here of the invigorating *élan* of the other comedies. Significantly, despite the fact that its settings are far removed from those of normal society (military HQ, hostels, troopship), this is of all Hawks's films the one that makes the closest contact with the realities of the modern world: it is the darkest of his comedies, and the one that gains most from being seen in the context of the adventure films. Its oppressive atmosphere contrasts strikingly with the exhilarating freshness, the sense of uncluttered freedom, that characterises the extra-social groups of the adventure films. It isn't a matter of *physical* constriction: the men in the (more or less) besieged jail of *Rio Bravo* are spiritually and emotionally freer than the characters of *I Was a Male War Bride*.

The film uses its satire on the bureaucracy of the military machine to attack certain characteristic trends of modern America. At the beginning European muddle sets off American super-efficiency: Henri cannot learn the way to Heidelberg from either his German driver or the civilians the driver questions. While they frantically contradict each other, Henri leans out and asks an American soldier, who tells him with quiet precision. This image of America is sustained throughout the film, notably through the character of Lieutenant Catherine Gates (Ann Sheridan) who accompanies Henri on his mission and accomplishes it for him while he is in prison owing to a misunderstanding which she deliberately omits to clear up. The film is chiefly concerned with the corollary of this efficiency: ruthlessness, total lack of flexibility, tendency to treat human beings as stereotypes. If the film falls into two halves, in the first of which Henri is up against the American female, in the second the whole bureaucratic machine, it is not broken-backed; both are depicted as the product of the same national tendency. Lieutenant Gates is Hawks's extremest and most explicit portrait of the modern American female, aggressive and domineering, determinedly subjugating the male. With this

I Was a Male War Bride: Captain and Madame Rochard (Cary Grant and Ann Sheridan)

goes an extreme sexual prudishness: she is reluctant even to allow Henri to rub her back. It is one of the strengths of the film that we are made to register all this as a matter of conditioned response, while we are repeatedly made aware of the character's submerged femininity.

The pivot of the film is the scene culminating in Henri's and Catherine's discovery that they aren't going to have a wedding-night, at least not together. Hawks and his players convey, in a minute or so, the sense of a mature relationship developing, a mutual tenderness and respect, with a much-mellowed Catherine. Certain sequences in the first half of the film point forward to this: the moments of direct physical contact (Henri rubbing her back), where we become aware of Catherine as a woman, beneath the military uniform and the puritanical manner; the excursions into natural surroundings, culminating in the beautiful and funny scene in the middle of a haystack where the two characters' mutual attraction is mutually acknowledged. After the wedding-night scene, when officialdom takes over, Catherine becomes again the militant female, gloating over her husband's discomfitures. The one central scene 'places' all that precedes and all that follows.

I Was a Male War Bride pushes furthest the sexual reversal characteristic of Hawksian comedy. Henri's progress as an 'alien spouse of female military personnel en route to the United States under Public Law 271', from the moment when he learns he is eligible to travel as his wife's bride, leads inevitably to the actual assumption of female disguise. The process gives opportunities for Hawks's funniest sex-reversal jokes: Henri, in a room full of war brides, listens to the fashion news coming over the loudspeaker system and, on learning that the 'natural bust-line' is returning, surreptitiously transfers his wallet to his hip pocket. Yet one is never in doubt as to the character's masculinity. Henri has a resilience characteristic of the Hawks hero, whether in adventure film or comedy. When, during his nocturnal search for somewhere to sleep, he starts learning to knit with the girl at the enquiry desk of one of the 'female buildings', there is no loss of male dignity. By means of his sardonic humour and emotional balance and maturity, he preserves his sanity and manliness to the end.

The difference between Henri Rochard and the heroes of the adventure films is purely environmental. The charming scene between Henri and the private from Brooklyn, with its warm intuitive sympathy, takes us into the atmosphere of the adventure films and their male groups. Henri is quite distinct from the heroes of the other comedies. The disasters that befall the protagonists of *Bringing up Baby, Monkey Business, Man's Favourite Sport?,* and *Scarface* are directly related to weaknesses or lacks in their own characters. In Henri, a protagonist from Hawks's adventure films is transplanted into an environment he isn't equipped to cope with: but it is the environment, not the character, that is intrinsically 'wrong'. Henri is the Hawks hero isolated. In nearly all the adventure films the hero operates within a more or less unified group, to which he gives strength but from which he also derives it. Henri has no support beyond his own resource and resilience.

The humiliations Henri undergoes culminate logically not only

in female disguise (in which he looks, if anything, more masculine than ever) but also in imprisonment (in the ship's cabin). As the film continues, more and more restrictions are imposed by the bureaucratic regulations in which American 'efficiency' manifests itself, and movement becomes increasingly constricted. The irony of the concluding shot of the Statue of Liberty (as seen from Henri's cabin-cell) is its final masterstroke and perhaps the nearest thing in Hawks to overt comment on modern society.

4: The Group

Hawks and Ford, *Air Force* (1943), *Ball of Fire* (1941), *The Thing from Another World* (1951)

Hawks and Ford

No two Hawks groups are quite the same—they are too much composed of individuals—and the nature of the group often differs radically from film to film. *Red Line 7000* shows it at its loosest and most heterogeneous. The men simply happen to have similar interests and ambitions. There is more antagonism in the group than togetherness, and none of those intense male friendships and mutural admirations that form within the groups of most of the adventure films (*Only Angels Have Wings, Rio Bravo, Hatari!*, etc.). At the other extreme is *Air Force*, where group unity becomes the central theme. Between these extremes are those variously loose assemblages of human beings that constitute the majority of Hawks's groups.

The group environment is not essential to that friendship between men so common in Hawks's work: in *A Girl in Every Port* both men are sailors, but their friendship isn't tied to any group feeling, and, although there is a group in *The Big Sky*, the friendship between Kirk Douglas and Dewey Martin is quite independent of it. Nor is the group essential to the definition of the Hawksian hero: that Bogart in *To Have and Have Not* is the purest embodiment of the values Hawks's heroes represent is partly due to the fact that he exists in isolation, without ties beyond the purely personal. The only common factor is that these groups, loosely formed and fluctuating, offer an alternative to (or an escape from?) the organised modern society in which the comedies are nominally set.

Hawks's groups contrast with those in John Ford's cavalry Westerns. The theme of *She Wore a Yellow Ribbon* is the relationship of the individual to the cavalry troop and its traditions. The emphasis is on the need for submission to a discipline. The men—and the women (the education of Olivia Dandridge in becoming an 'army wife' is a leading thematic and narrative thread)—are defined by their allegiance to an established code of behaviour. The tradition—which offers a definition of manhood that includes loyalty, gallantry, and personal initiative side by side with courtesy and consideration for women as the representatives of the civilised values—ennobles all who subscribe to its influence and disciplines. Consider the film's memorable scenes—the operation in the moving wagon during the thunderstorm, with the Major's wife singing 'Round her leg she wore a yellow garter' with the wounded man; the death and burial of General (or Trooper) Clay; the presentation of the silver watch to Captain Brittles on his retirement—and this sense of the tradition and the values it embodies will quickly be felt as an all-pervading influence, determining the tone and *feel* of the film.

There is nothing of this in Hawks: the idea of tradition seems not to exist for him. Ford's cavalrymen, like Conrad's sailors, are referred back to the traditions of the service to which they belong; in *Air Force* the group loyalty, and loyalty to the plane that unifies the group, develops spontaneously between the men and the machine: there is no sense that the men are being formed by values sanctioned by an accumulated tradition. The soldiers in *The Thing from Another World* are a group of men who happen to be soldiers; the characters of *She Wore a Yellow Ribbon* are cavalrymen first, individuals second. All of Hawks's groups are *ad hoc* collections of individuals who remain individuals first and foremost; their responsibilities are to personal ties.

In an age when the sense of traditions is collapsing, it is inevitable that Hawks, whose work shows little sense of the past and whose characters live in and for the present, seems the more modern artist. It is significant that the prevalent emotion in Ford's Westerns is nostalgia, and that it is so difficult, in his work, to distinguish the valid response to valid ideals from sentimentality. But the advantage is certainly not all on Hawks's side. What one misses in his work consistently—it is strongly present in Ford's—is a sense of the potentialities of civilisation. He is a primitive: or more precisely, a curious mixture of the primitive and the sophisticated, which is why the relationship between the two is such a conspicuous feature of his work (*Bringing up Baby, Monkey Business, Hatari!*). As such he has his own particular strengths: the importance in his work of the spontaneous and instinctive, the emphasis on physical contact and physical experience. It is true of most artists that their strengths carry attendant limitations.

What one registers as a permanent immaturity in Hawks—the inability to come to grips with modern civilisation—goes hand in hand with the maturity of his heroes. A favourable condition for the existence of their maturity is the absence of organised society; which suggests that the maturity is somewhat limited. It remains, however, within the limitations, a perfectly valid concept. The maturity lies in the man's inner freedom from constraints, his ability to trust his own spontaneous impulses of attraction and repulsion; in his achieved sense of identity, based on a defining of his responsibilities and allegiances; in his preservation of independence. The Hawks hero, typically, is committed to nothing beyond the preservation of his self-respect and any personal ties he chooses to acknowledge. The ideal environment for maturity thus conceived is a society more informal, less stratified—in fact more *primitive*—than our own, a society in which the maximum possible freedom co-exists with the minimum necessary security. The Hawks group always has a leader, but he is more a benevolent father-figure (Wayne in *Rio Bravo* and *Hatari!* is the perfect example) than a dictator: in several films he is addressed as 'Papa'. When he becomes a dictator, as in *Red River*, the group eschews him. He is always a natural leader, neither elected nor imposed, holding his position purely because he embodies the Hawksian maturity more completely than anybody else. He is more an example to be followed than a commander: a touchstone against which success and failure can be measured. Despite the presence of this leader-figure, one's chief impression is of a society without a government: the laws are natural laws that are learnt through experience (as Colorado learns responsibility in *Rio Bravo*), not commandments imposed from on high. The recurring pattern (*A Girl in Every Port*, *Red River*, *The Big Sky*, *Hatari!*) of a relationship beginning in hostility and rivalry and passing through exchanged blows or some kind of trial such as target-shooting to mutual acceptance and respect, comes to look like ritual, and one is tempted to talk in terms of clubs and initiation ceremonies; to do so is misleading, because such 'initiation' is always treated in purely personal terms, never as a condition of group membership. What almost gets Chips (Gérard Blain) excluded from the group in *Hatari!* is the suspicion that he is meanly self-seeking, lacking the outgoing impulses which vital relationship demands. There is no rigid test of manhood: Pockets (Red Buttons), who is terrified of animals and incapable of fighting anyone, is a fully accepted member of the hunters' society in *Hatari!* Within the group, one feels an absence of *civilised* sensibility, but the strong presence of the uncultivated, instinctive sensibility that must underlie any valid civilisation: intuitive-sympathetic contact, a sturdily positive, generous spirit.

Air Force

Hawks seems little interested in *Air Force:* it is scarcely alluded to in his fairly inclusive interviews. It was, we are told, his 'contribution to the war effort'. I approached it with little enthusiasm, expecting at best an efficient, external war film. It proved to be one of his greatest works: in feeling perhaps the noblest.

It is less completely personal than, say, *Only Angels Have Wings* only in that it is less typical; if one made a parody of Hawks, *Air Force* would be almost untouched by it. None the less, only Hawks could have made it. It bears an essential relationship to the 'typical' films, is superior to some (for instance, *Hatari!*); and is informed by a deep commitment. The imposed situation—the action exclusively concerning a bomber and its crew—seems to have acted as a discipline, supplying Hawks with a congenial theme while withholding opportunities of introducing the characters and situations that recur in the mainstream films.

Air Force has the perfect proportion one finds in so many of Hawks's films. It is built up on a cumulative rhythm of alternation (flights alternating with episodes on various Pacific islands) moving steadily to the climax. I have had to take that climax on trust: though promised in the official synopsis and referred to in contemporary reviews, it is inexplicably missing from the copy in the British Film Archive. The main body of the film is framed between two corresponding moments: the first when, after the news of the attack on Pearl Harbor has been received over the radio, planes of the air fleet diverge; the second when the Mary Ann, after accidentally sighting a Japanese fleet, joins another force of bombers and guides them to the attack for the Battle of the Coral Sea. We never entirely lose sight of the Mary Ann's function as a single unit of a vast organism; but between those two moments she is alone. This principle of single-units-of-a-vast-organism is basic to the film. We watch the integration of the individual into the crew of the Mary Ann; the integration of the Mary Ann into the large force; and the film ends with preparations for a massed attack on Tokyo.

The Mary Ann becomes a symbol of preserved order—preserved by teamwork to which each individual contributes—in a chaotic world. The internal order within the plane, with its accompanying sense of security, is played off against shots of the desolated, bombed airfields on which the plane lands, improvised beacons flaring through the darkness, menacing jungle all round. By stressing its basis in the realistic and the practical, Hawks purges the idealism of the men's feeling for their plane of any suggestion of sentimentality. The plane is the focus of loyalty that unifies the group.

The opening scene of farewell—the Captain's goodbye to his wife, his meeting with the mother of the very young crew-member —has in its simplicity an intensity that evokes Dunson's parting from Fen at the beginning of *Red River*. Though brief, it links the men with a stable background of civilised emotions, from which they are cut off for the remainder of the film. They carry their civilisation with them, in their own miniature society. Two small reminders of civilised values are carried within the Mary Ann: the mascot-toy sent by the Captain's small son, and the dog Tripoli, picked up on Wake Island. One is struck here by the total absence of sentimentality in Hawks's treatment of ideas that positively encourage it. The 'charm' neither saves the Captain's life nor is used to make a poignant-ironic point when he dies—it remains merely a concrete reminder of what has been left behind. Tripoli is handed to Corporal Weinberg (George Tobias) by the marines on Wake Island who know (and the crew of the Mary Ann know it too) that they will never get off. The dog is the sole remaining focus for emotions associated with home and peacetime, and the solicitude of the crew for him is much more than sentimentality over one small animal.

The crew of the Mary Ann are less strongly individualised than is usual with Hawks's characters: their separate identities merge into their group identity. The relative evaluation of individualism and group responsibility, with the possibility of reconciling the two to their mutual benefit, is principally developed through the rear-gunner Winocki (John Garfield). The central thread of the first half of *Air Force* is Winocki's integration into the group. At the beginning, his determination to preserve independence is reinforced by a personal grudge against the Captain, who before the take-off tells him 'We all belong to this aeroplane. Every man has got to rely on every other man to do the right thing at the right time.' Against Winocki is set the Mary Ann's navigator, son of a famous flier, who wanted to be a pilot but who accepts his role as a unit of the group, and whose personal triumph comes when he finds the airfield on Wake Island through almost impenetrable storm-clouds.

Winocki's individualism is at first aggressive and destructive; we trace the process, not of its suppression, but of its conversion into a positive force. It is Winocki who accepts responsibility for smuggling Tripoli on board, making explicit what the dog means to everyone: the self-styled outcast becomes a spokesman for the values of the crew. The integration which follows carries for Winocki a sense of fulfilment: far from losing integrity, he gains it. That fulfilment finds its expression in action when the plane is hit and the Captain mortally wounded. The crew bale out, Winocki remains—against orders—and brings plane and captain to the ground, in a crash-landing. Winocki has achieved his ambition to be a pilot, but the personal ambition has been assimilated into something nobler: it is the triumph of individualism placed at the service of something beyond itself, plane and Captain constituting the focal point of group unity. Despite its officially hierarchic nature, the crew appears an ideal democracy in microcosm: the atmosphere is one of voluntary service, of discipline freely accepted; a perfect balance is achieved between individual fulfilment and the responsibility of each member to the whole. The crew *enact* the values they are fighting for.

Winocki is the centre of the film's moment of maximum intensity: the scene where a young flier is machine-gunned by an enemy fighter-pilot, first as he hangs, defenceless, in mid-air from the straps of his parachute, then as, gravely wounded, parachute still attached, he tries to crawl to cover. The sequence is given us through Winocki's consciousness: he watches, and it is he who brings down the fighter and 'executes'—we feel it as that—the pilot as he struggles out. An eye for an eye, and very horrible; yet behind the action there is so powerful an accumulation of moral outrage that one accepts it. Reduced to intellectual ideas, the scene is banal: a man sees something horrible, feels revulsion, is spurred to violent reprisal. In terms of the communication of feeling, it is intensely moving: we see a hitherto unthinking man reach, through instinctive reaction, conscious moral awareness, and we share with him, through the force of the images, the experience of reaching it. The whole film, and particularly this scene, have doubtless benefited from the time-lapse since *Air Force* was made. The superficial level of anti-Japanese propaganda, presumably taken for granted in 1943, now seems almost entirely

Air Force: the machine-gunning of the parachutist →

illusory, and the real theme emerges, stripped of all nationalistic pettiness. Even the climactic bombing of the Japanese fleet comes across in its context more as the logical symbolic culmination of a dramatic poem about the group than as the expression of nationalist feeling.

Every scene in the film is informed by Hawks's concept of the group built on shared values, common purpose, intuitive sympathy, and mutual dependence. Three sequences stand out. The first is the scene in which (on arrival at Manila) the Crew Chief (Harry Carey) receives the news of his son's death, and his few pitiful surviving belongings wrapped in a handkerchief. It provides the only moment in *Air Force* that directly recalls another Hawks film, in the father's comment, 'Not much to show for twenty years' (compare *Only Angels Have Wings*). The effect here is even more poignant than in the earlier film, because of our awareness of the man's feelings about the son: the pride of a man who in middle age is still a sergeant in the son who at twenty is already a lieutenant (the actor beautifully conveys humiliation without resentment, and a sense that he is fulfilling through the boy the ambitions he had for himself). No softening is allowed: the boy didn't die a hero, he 'didn't even get off the ground'. Then, abruptly, as the father stands holding the handkerchief, a raid begins, the Mary Ann must be got off the ground, private grief is submerged in group action.

Any attempt to describe the sequence of Captain Quincannon's death will make it sound insufferably sentimental; its apparent excesses are carried, magnificently, by the intensity of feeling generated and by our awareness of its logic as one of the film's culminating expressions of group feeling (according to Hawks, the scene was written by William Faulkner). The Captain dies in a hospital bed surrounded by his crew, believing that the Mary Ann (condemned as beyond repair) is taking off with them all aboard. Gradually the crew fall in with the illusion, each man acting his role in the group, until the Navigator is asked for the direction ('Due east—into the sunrise') and the Captain dies. The death scene becomes a group ritual. One cannot talk of sentimentality when emotion and meaning are so beautifully integrated into the total structure.

The third scene—a long sequence interrupted by the incident of the machine-gunning of the parachutist—is the film's supreme achievement (unless the missing climax outdoes it): the rebuilding, against orders, of the Mary Ann by its crew, with spare parts stolen from other wrecks. The intensity of this scene derives from several sources. There is the controlled suspense of the fight against time: the plane must be off the ground before the Japanese reach the airfield, or the crew must blow it up. The suspense is tightened in a tremendous *accelerando*: as the Japanese break out of the jungle, the explosives are in readiness, and Weinberg, on the nose, is still tightening the last propeller screw as the plane is moved into position for take-off. The context of the scene is important, following the Captain's death: the death-take-off was a lie, the lie must be made truth. Above all the scene is the supreme example of group expression. With the resurrection of the plane, as the focus for loyalties, the group can survive the death of its leader. The scene is profoundly stirring, the men's fervour spreading so that the group attracts others to its aid like a magnet, the marines forming a human chain to refuel the engines. When the Mary Ann takes off, it is piloted by Lieutenant Rader, the fighter-pilot who earlier scoffed at the 'responsibility' and 'dependence' of work in a bomber.

The original film ends—apparently—with a crash-landing on an Australian beach and a new Mary Ann serving as focal point for the same crew-members, setting out in the massed attack on Tokyo. This gives, clearly, a further 'resurrection', and shows the group surviving not only its Captain but its unifying centre.

Air Force has a flawless thematic logic that entirely overcomes one's resistance to an action often far-fetched. It communicates a magnificently realised sense of fulfilment and wholeness, and deserves to become a permanent classic of the American cinema.

Ball of Fire

While more typical of the comedies than *Air Force* is of the

Air Force: the rebuilding of the Mary Ann →

adventure films, *Ball of Fire* is not fully representative (like *Air Force*, it gets neglected in Hawks's interviews). It hasn't quite the *élan* of most of the comedies, nor their qualities of excess, despite its extravagant basic situation (gangster's moll hides out in home of eight bachelor professors single-mindedly dedicated to work on an exhaustive encyclopedia, on the pretext of helping them in their researches into slang). Its unusual gentleness is perfectly suited to its essential subject.

Its most obvious relationship is to *Bringing up Baby*: it could almost have been made to right the imbalances of the earlier film. Again the favourite Hawksian clash of opposite worlds: on the one hand a world of serious (even when absurd) dedication to learning, on the other a world of total irresponsibility. Only this time the film comes down firmly—though not without qualifications—on the side of culture and dedication, with the barbarians unequivocally routed. The decisive factor—in terms of the director's sympathies—is the presence of Hawks's oddest group.

What surprises from the outset is the weight given to the dedication. Hawks never allows its seriousness to be affected by the characters' endearing absurdity. The professors are conceived in comic terms that verge on caricature; yet when Miss Totten's solicitor, trying to get the encyclopedia pushed to its conclusion without further expenditure, tells them to 'Slap it together', we register the words as brutally insensitive. In a later scene, the gangsters' shooting-up of the professors' house just for the hell of it comes across as totally unfunny. The feeling is of pure moral outrage: we are far here from the insidious involvement in anarchy of *Scarface*.

Hawks distinguishes firmly between the absurdity of the characters and the seriousness of their work. The professors wander in the park for their lunch-break, together, yet entirely separate, all talking, yet each in his own world, the field in which he is a specialist. Break over, they return to the house and to the encyclopedia, and immediately the barriers break down, and they cohere as a group. Separately, each is absurd; united in group activity, they take on dignity. The housekeeper, Miss Bragg, is a formidable, bossy mother-figure, the professors absurd children: Professor Oddly (Richard Haydn) has stolen a pot of jam and has to be reprimanded. But the moment any conflict arises over their work, they are the masters—they grow up, and order Miss Bragg about peremptorily. It is not only a matter of dedication. When Oddly steals a pot of jam he is an individual; when their work is threatened they are a group.

From the introduction of Sugarpuss, the central thread of the film becomes not so much a conflict between two worlds as their mutual improvement through interaction. Sugarpuss's crude, sensual vitality stimulates the professors' capacity for spontaneous enjoyment; the professors' innocence and gentleness develop in Sugarpuss a rudimentary conscience and sensitivity. Sugarpuss's primitive, if vulgarised, energy apart, Hawks here allows no virtues to the representatives of irresponsibility. The gangsters are presented as complacent and brutish; the feeling of the film, in the scenes where Bertram Potts (Gary Cooper) is progressively duped and humiliated by them is very pure: we are never invited to laugh at Bertram, only—and then uneasily—at the situations.

This purity of feeling manifests itself in the smallest details of the *mise-en-scène*. When Joe Lilac (Dana Andrews) strikes Cooper's face and punches him in the belly (Cooper bears traces of Sugarpuss's lipstick), he chucks a lighted cigarette at the dining-table where the other professors are still seated. Professor Robinson (Tully Marshall) drops it with an off-hand, almost unconscious and instinctive contempt in a coffee-cup, so that it won't mark the table. The gesture (done quite unobtrusively: Hawks never cuts in to close-up for such things) beautifully expresses the civilised values that place the gangsters' vicious vandalism. The attitude to learning in general, and the treatment of the Cooper character in particular, consistently reverses the pattern of feeling in *Bringing up Baby*. In *Ball of Fire* the movement of the comedy is more constructive. It lacks something of the earlier film's flashes of crazy invention but it is more balanced, and fundamentally more sensitive.

The balance between the primitive and the civilised is satisfying

Ball of Fire: Sugarpuss and the Professors

and beautiful. The professors' final triumph over the gangsters, and Bertram's subsequent winning of Sugarpuss, are the result of an alliance of learning and animal instinct. History and Science (the sword of Damocles and Archimedes' use of reflected light) are evoked to defeat the gang who are holding the professors at gunpoint to force the converted Sugarpuss to marry her one-time hero. But there comes a time in any Hawks film where learning gives way to something more basic. Bertram, on the way to rescue Sugarpuss, studies an ancient boxing manual. Joe knocks him down contemptuously, Bertram throws the book aside and falls back on pure instinctive indignation: Joe is soundly beaten. The pattern is repeated in the last scene. Previously, Professor Magenbruch (S. Z. Sakall) has correctly interpreted Sugarpuss's mistake in sending Bertram the wrong ring in terms of Freud's theory of errors. All the professors unite to convince her of the rightness of marrying Bertram, with examples drawn from History,

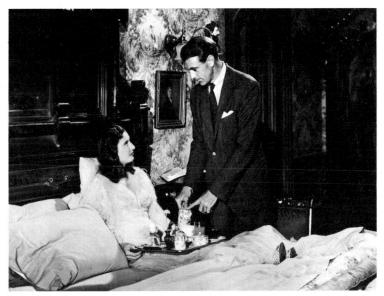

Ball of Fire: Sugarpuss and Professor Potts

Geography, Literature; then Bertram kisses her. She capitulates.

The sensitivity with which Hawks treats culture in this film is related to his response to the idea of the group. The final triumph is a group triumph; the group is consistently felt to be behind Cooper. When he announces his engagement to Sugarpuss, they *all* kiss her, with the comment, 'We feel you're marrying all of us.' Cooper looks on at their participation with evident pleasure: though he has acted independently, he values the group's approval. The most beautiful scene in the film—so good it survives transplantation, more or less intact, into *A Song is Born*, Hawks's vastly inferior remake of *Ball of Fire* with Danny Kaye and Virginia Mayo—is the sequence of the bachelor party on the night before Cooper's anticipated wedding. Sugarpuss withdraws sadly; embroiled in her relationship with Joe, she sees in the group an innocence from which she is excluded. The ensuing scene uses the tradition of the bachelor party, without any of its traditional coarseness, to suggest that Cooper is being given a group blessing: informal ritual again plays its part. In the marriage reminiscences of Professor Oddly (the only widower in the group) Hawks beautifully balances the absurd and the poignant: there is touching tenderness for the past, and for the dead Genevieve, co-existing with ludicrous timidity ('I kissed her hand each night, astonished at my own boldness'). Throughout the speech, Cooper is pre-occupied with his own imminent (and very different) marriage, and the two become juxtaposed when Oddly produces a lock of Genevieve's hair which still, he says, looks as if the sunlight were in it (seeing Sugarpuss with the sunlight in her hair first made Cooper aware of his feelings for her). The men sing 'Genevieve, sweet Genevieve', as a group tribute to Oddly; cut to a shot of Sugarpuss alone in her room, brooding and disturbed, the song from across the courtyard—again juxtaposing the two very different women, living and dead. Oddly retires, asking them to go on singing 'Genevieve'. The communal singing expresses group solidarity, group nostalgia—Oddly's nostalgia, here experienced vicariously by the whole group—and regret at lost youth and all they have missed (all that Bertram, they believe, is to have, for them another vicarious experience). 'Genevieve' gives way to 'Gaudeamus igitur', which, off-screen, accompanies Bertram as he goes to ask Oddly's advice about marriage. Bertram, however, goes to the wrong room: in the dark, he makes his speech, intended for Oddly, to Sugarpuss: a speech about the relative impurity of his feelings for his bride. Sugarpuss gets up and embraces him: she has found a man who offers her a *complete* love. Cooper's seriousness is given great weight in the scene.

I have described this sequence in detail to try to suggest the richness and complexity of the feeling it communicates. Essential to that richness is the sense of contact, of tenderness communicated and experience shared through sympathy, that springs from the presence of the group, felt through the singing even when the characters are off-screen. *Ball of Fire* may not be the most vivid of Hawks's comedies, but it is an intensely personal film whose mellowness earns it a special place in one's affections.

The Thing from Another World: finding the Flying Saucer

The Thing from Another World

The Thing was directed by Christian Nyby, Hawks's editor in
Red River and other films; Hawks prepared the script and super-
vised the production. No one who has seen it can doubt that in all
essentials it is a Hawks film. Not only the perfection of its structure
and its close thematic relevance but the whole style of the direction
itself (the treatment of dialogue, for example, with that rapid
overlapping technique developed by Hawks in the comedies)
unmistakably expresses Hawks's personality. Beside Hawks's
masterpiece, *The Thing* is a minor work, but much of the *feel* of
Rio Bravo is there, if in miniature. There is the almost exclusively
male group, and the group feeling. There is the Hawksian woman
(Margaret Sheridan), the equal of any man, yet intensely feminine.
And there is the sense of isolation from any established society.
There is also the austere and comfortless setting (in *Rio Bravo* a
jail, here a few Nissen huts in the Arctic wastes), fitting background
to Hawks's stoicism. But here there is another, larger context, a

new perspective: outer space. For all the strength and resilience of the characters, with their characteristic warmth, their admirable resourcefulness, the scene where the men spread themselves out on the ice to discover the shape of the space-ship and find themselves forming a perfect circle chillingly conveys the sense of man's smallness and helplessness in a vast and mysterious universe. Who but Hawks, who in *Monkey Business* treated man's innate subversive primitivism as a subject for riotous comedy, could counter the feelings of terror induced here with so firm a sense of humour and lightness of spirit?

The scene is complex in tone; the flexible groupings, mostly in medium- or long-shot, keep various contrasted characters—soldiers, scientists, journalist—and their contrasted reactions before us simultaneously, held in balance against each other, and the dread is qualified by a continual play of humour. Scotty, the journalist, is very exactly realised: he is treated with sympathy but at the same time with a consistent irony. His responses invariably take the form of slogans in current journalese: he breaks the awed amazement at the discovery of the space-ship's shape with an enthusiastic cry of 'We've found a flying saucer!' The Thing is to him an 'intellectual carrot' ('the mind boggles!')—when it has ceased to be a 'Man from Mars'. His final warning to 'Watch the skies' is a good example of the exactness of touch Hawks achieves. It is perfectly in character, and in line with Scotty's other clichés: behind him, as he broadcasts, stand three of the soldiers, striking modest-heroic poses with a comic effect the greater for being understated. But it also points to the essential terrors underlying the habitual tone of light comedy: the precariousness of Man's position in the universe, at the mercy of whatever forces may be Out There. We have seen what one Thing can do, and grasped the speed with which it can multiply; what about a hundred Things? A thousand. . . .

Considered purely as an example of the fifties cycle of films about flying saucers and invasions from space, *The Thing* has several distinguishing characteristics. The *raison d'être* of most SF movies is to provide a field-day for the special effects department: in *The*

Thing there are no superimpositions, no inflated mechanical monsters cavorting on one strip of film while human beings shriek and gesticulate on another. In technique it is simple and rigorous, depending for its suspense and its shocks partly on its construction (the alternation of long and leisurely build-ups and very brief explosions of violence again evokes *Rio Bravo*), partly on timing so perfectly judged that after repeated viewings one still jumps, partly on the directness and honesty of the staging of each scene. James Arness, The Thing itself, staggers round a room blazing while the other actors, with characteristic Hawksian abandon, fling kerosene over him, and we see the flinging and the blazing in the same shot. The chief effect of this technical simplicity is to direct our attention where it belongs and where, in SF movies, it seldom goes, to the characters and, through them, to the film's essential concerns.

In most SF films the characters are bloodless stereotypes; one's sympathies are all with the monster or the invading force and one is very disheartened when it is wiped out (a point of which a few, but only a few, films have made expressive use: *King Kong* is the obvious example). *The Thing* gives us some grounds for caring about the survival of the human race. This helps the film enormously on the 'thriller' level; but, more than this, it is essential to its deeper concerns. The characterisation is not psychologically detailed, having the simplicity befitting a parable. What makes the characters live is the human values they embody. The affection of the characters for each other reflects that which Hawks feels for them: an affection warm but unidealising, dignified by respect. In the scenes between the soldiers there is a continual sense of living human beings responding to one another with an intuitive awareness the scientists largely lack. There is nothing profound or remarkable in their dialogue, which is mostly on the level of amusing chaff; the effect is conveyed through that relaxed but mutually responsive acting typical of Hawks's films, on which the sense of mutual sympathy (in its root sense of *feeling together*) is built.

Hawks's affection for human beings finds its clearest embodiment

The Thing from Another World: Captain Hendrey and Nikki

in the film in the relationship between Captain Hendrey and Nikki, Professor Carrington's secretary. Far from being the usual bit of perfunctory love interest, this is an economically sketched Hawksian man-woman relationship, which perfectly fulfils an important function.

The central conflict in *The Thing* is not between humanity and a destructive invader, but between two opposed concepts of value embodied in the two opposed groups whose clash the Thing precipitates. To Professor Carrington (Robert Cornthwaite) knowledge is the only aim worth living for, its pursuit the justification for man's existence. Man is constantly retarded in this aim by all that part of his nature that he shares with the animals: sexuality and emotions. To Carrington the Thing, vegetable, reproducing itself by dropping seeds from the palms of its hands, capable of neither pleasure nor pain, and evidencing, through its space-ship, an intellectual development enormously in advance of mankind's, becomes an ideal, to be preserved at all costs, even that of humanity: if it is superior beyond comparison to mankind, hasn't it the right to use men as we use, say cattle?

Carrington's position has the strength of a reasoned case. Captain Hendrey, his chief opponent, has nothing behind him but instinct, and the background of human warmth and spontaneity represented by the soldiers. The Thing does indeed use men as we use cattle (hangs them upside-down with their throats cut like carcasses in a slaughterhouse and drains their blood); it must at all costs be destroyed. There is more here than mere self-preservation. It is human relationships that, to Hendrey as to Hawks, give life its value, the vital intercourse between human beings: affection and respect, love and friendship. The Thing represents a logical extension of all Carrington stands for: without emotions but with a great intellect, it can have nothing to live for but the pursuit of knowledge. As he says of it admiringly, 'No pleasure, no pain . . . no emotions. . . . Our superior in every way.'

There is no question which side the film is on: it upholds the development to maturity of the whole human being as against that of the intellect in isolation. Its relationship to certain of Hawks's comedies, notably *Bringing up Baby* and *Monkey Business* (where Cornthwaite's reappearance as a scientist draws attention to the connection), is clear. While remaining so different in mood and overt subject-matter, the three films are linked by their implication of the failure of scientific interests to develop and mature the whole personality. It is the tendency of the scientific outlook to inhibit emotional development that makes possible Barnaby Fulton's escape into total irresponsibility (*Monkey Business*) and is at the root of all the humiliations undergone by David Huxley (*Bringing up Baby*); a by no means negligible subject in a world becoming increasingly science-orientated.

But *The Thing*'s strength derives partly from its fairness to the other side. Carrington—while he is the perfect opponent of everything Hawks, with his 'primitive' feeling for spontaneity and instinct, stands for—is never made absurd: he is on the contrary consistently presented as intelligent, dedicated, and courageous, willing to die for his beliefs. There are some beautiful moments in

Cornthwaite's performance, behind which we sense Hawks's respect for professionalism in whatever cause: the humility with which he apologises to Hendrey for the vagueness of his information about the unidentified flying object; the sense of humiliation when he admits that he, with his pride in his intellect, is no more impressive or useful to the Thing than a cabbage is to us. The climax of the film gains great intensity by this determination to keep us aware of the strength of the opposite position. The Thing, when at last we see it clearly, loses much of its terror. In medium long-shot and from a medium-high angle, it ceases to look huge, and its close likeness to a human being (the human being of a future to which Carrington looks forward) becomes evident. (I can't imagine why people find this a *weakness* of the film: do they *really* want a goggle-eyed robot?) The impossibility of communication becomes almost poignant—it looks as if it would be so easy to talk to. It is destroyed: we watch a marvellous, if terrible, being reduced to a small pile of smouldering ashes, on which the camera lingers to allow the spectator a complex reaction: we have been made to respect Carrington's viewpoint sufficiently for us to find the outcome a triumph not unqualified, a reaction shared by the characters on the screen, who stand by in stunned silence. We also realise that Hawks's position here is not the simple anti-intellectual one that could be read into *Bringing up Baby*: the Thing has been destroyed by science. One of the points that emerges is that science is for man's use—Carrington's viewpoint would turn everything topsy-turvy, making man the servant of science.

Finally, to compare with the above account there is Hawks's own. Asked by Peter Bogdanovich whether he was criticising scientists in *The Thing*, he replied: 'Oh no, it just worked out that way. You see, we had to make it plausible—why they let the Thing live.'

5: Male Relationships

A Girl in Every Port (1928), *The Big Sky* (1952), *Come and Get It* (1936), *Red River* (1948)

A Girl in Every Port, The Big Sky

A Girl in Every Port is the first example in Hawks's work of 'a love story between two men'; it points forward especially to *The Big Sky*. The early film is the more fully realised: but *The Big Sky* is the more interesting and it has by far the more acceptable resolution.

Dissatisfaction with *A Girl in Every Port* centres upon a 'happy ending' in which the characters remain arrested at an immature stage of development. Bill (Robert Armstrong), a lady-killer with conquests all over the world, and a compulsive need to establish ownership by affixing his mark (a tattooed heart and anchor) to them, appears to lose interest in girls as soon as his relationship with Spike (Victor McLaglen) is established. They get drunk together, after cementing their union by pushing a policeman into the water; Spike shows interest in a girl in the bar, and Bill repeatedly picks fights to distract Spike's attention from her and keep it on himself. Bill's lack of feeling for women becomes clearer still when Spike expresses the need to settle down: Bill sees women only as 'sexy skirts' and he can't understand why anyone should jump ship for one.

The character clearly anticipates Boone in *The Big Sky*; but Boone's position in the relationship is more firmly defined, his immaturity placed and eventually transcended. The ending of *A Girl in Every Port*, with its total—and cursorily handled—

exclusion of the woman from the men's lives, comes across oddly, given the spirit in which it is offered. Not only is the men's friendship—permanently, apparently—confirmed by excluding women (and Spike, at least, seems to need them); the relationship itself hasn't undergone any significant development, arrested at a level of jolly fisticuffs. Probably it couldn't have been deepened without acknowledgement—both on the men's part and on Hawks's —of its strong homosexual undertones, and much of the film's charm lies in its innocence. This resolution never again satisfied Hawks; the ending of *The Big Sky* is not only more complex and subtle—it shows an altogether more mature awareness.

A secondary—and related—source of dissatisfaction is Hawks's failure to realise the potentialities of Louise Brooks. She might well have established the tradition of the Hawks woman, but, after a promising beginning, her part degenerates into a commonplace figure of female duplicity, simplifying the issues unfairly and making it impossible to use the actress's full resources.

The Big Sky is the least of Hawks's Westerns, as surely as *Rio Bravo* is the best. One only intermittently senses the depth and intensity of personal involvement that give *Red River* and *Rio Bravo* their concentrated significance. Hawks failed to achieve the right creative relationship with Kirk Douglas, and failed to realise the character of Teal Eye, the Indian girl: she is meant to be remote and mysterious, but one must feel that her creator understands her. However, the film is unmistakably Hawks's, especially in its treatment of the male relationship.

In *The Big Sky* Hawks places the complex relationships of the two men and a girl against the story of the first journey up the Missouri river by white men in a keel-boat; a major weakness is the looseness of the relationship between the personal story and the epic background. Like *Red River*, *The Big Sky* has as a leading theme a young man's growth to maturity; but whereas in *Red River* the stages in that growth were also stages in the cattle-trek, public and private developments coinciding, it is difficult to find any such close connection in *The Big Sky*. Hawks at times forces the two elements together, as in the episode of the boat accident where the two men rescue Teal Eye from drowning; but that one uses the words 'force together' suggests the lack of *organic* relationship. This structural looseness is partly offset by the marked rhythm of the film, which is also the rhythm of the characters' lives: the alternation of daytime scenes on the river with night scenes in camp, the former for the most part forwarding the public story, the latter the private.

That we are led away so often from the personal story partly explains why we never feel very intimately involved with the characters. The use of long-shot as a stylistic feature increases the detachment, but offers compensating advantages. In *The Big Sky* the actors haul a real keel-boat up a real river, and the audience can see this. As with the pyramid-building in *Land of the Pharaohs* the use of long-shot makes it impossible to fake anything, and emphasises the importance of the group, by showing actions intact as group activities; though this isn't treated deeply in *The Big Sky*. Finally, filming in long-shot beautifully captures the sense of men amidst the unknown: the shots of Indians along the banks ominously following the boat have a mysterious beauty.

But the personal story remains the most interesting feature of *The Big Sky*. Hawks has returned repeatedly to the subject of close relationship between men, and he himself is explicit in calling it 'love'. Love is clearly the word: see, for instance, Kirk Douglas and Dewey Martin in the saloon scene of *The Big Sky* singing 'Whisky, leave me alone' together. But one should be chary of the word 'homosexual': for many it has unpleasant connotations and the close male friendships of Hawks's films are invariably presented as thoroughly healthy and natural. Their essence is a deep and strong mutual respect. The nearest homosexual character is probably Kid in *Only Angels Have Wings*: Kid's devotion to Cary Grant is absolute, and he shows no interest in women at all. But this is untypical; usually this 'love between men' either co-exists with heterosexual love or (as in *The Big Sky*) finally yields to it. On this basic theme Hawks has worked many variations. Most frequently, but also less centrally in the films

The Big Sky: Jim Deakins and Boone

concerned, we have a relationship of equals (Montgomery Clift and John Ireland in *Red River*: Hardy Kruger and Gérard Blain in *Hatari!*); sometimes of extreme unequals, one of whom teaches and saves the other (Wayne and Martin in *Rio Bravo*). In *Red River* the central relationship (Wayne/Clift) is virtually one of father and son; in *The Big Sky* it is a relationship between elder and younger brothers. The Blackfoot Indian's scalp which Boone (Dewey Martin) perpetually carries around is (so Boone believes) the scalp of the Indian who killed his brother, who died, Uncle Zeb (Arthur Hunnicutt) tells Boone, 'when he was only a few years older than you are now'. When Zeb speaks the words, the camera is on him and Jim Deakins (Kirk Douglas): Jim has taken the brother's place.

Boone, for all his show of independence, continually reveals his need for an older man to model himself on. Zeb partly fills the role (Boone adopts his favourite exclamation, 'Well I'll be dogged'), but Jim fills it better: the gap between them is far less and he is roughly the age Boone's real brother was when he was killed. The pattern of behaviour is established in the saloon scene, which offers close parallels with the bar scene in *A Girl in Every Port*. Jim gets hold of a waitress and dances her round, Boone (who wants Jim to himself) pulls him away; Jim leans back against the bar and whoops at the girl and Boone promptly imitates him. A clearer example—and one that points forward more directly to the film's development—comes during the first night's camping on the banks of the Missouri. The Indian girl, Teal Eye (Elizabeth Threatt), has kept her face resolutely covered; Jim begins to talk of the need for women he feels when he gets into the wilds, and tells of a veiled woman he saw once who obsessed him until he'd seen her face. Whereupon *Boone*—who hates Indians and has so far shown only hostility and distaste towards her—pulls the blanket from Teal Eye's face. Throughout the film, Boone does either what he thinks Jim expects of him or what Jim wants to do himself. Jim falls in love with Teal Eye, so Boone 'marries' her. After the arrival at the Indian camp, Boone, bored and restless (and, like Bill in the earlier film, uneasy at his friend's attraction to the idea of settling down), suggests going hunting; but Jim 'has a reason to stick around' (Teal Eye); whereupon Boone, as if picking up a cue, immediately says, 'Maybe I have a reason to stick around, too.' He goes to Teal Eye's tent because that is what Jim wants to do. One might see in this a hint that Boone (without being consciously aware of any such motivation) is finding a way of preventing Jim from deserting him (as his real brother deserted him by getting killed): significantly Boone's love for Jim is expressing itself through self-identification.

The position of a woman in this male relationship was suggested in the saloon scene. As they sing together, Jim lets the girl in between them but it is Boone who offers her whisky: she has to accept them both. Teal Eye remains an enigmatic figure throughout (less a mysterious presence than a mere absence); yet one infers that, in different ways, she loves both men. They are so closely involved with each other that the woman becomes drawn to both. Her attraction to Boone expresses itself in a violent sex-antagonism that relates interestingly to other man-woman relationships in Hawks. Her method of curing the wound she herself has inflicted on him is delightedly to pour whisky into it: Zeb says she has 'got through two whole gallons in three days'. Her love for Jim expresses itself in a protective tenderness, particularly strong in the scene where, after he is wounded, she warms him by holding him to her—a gesture that has great force when one recalls her extreme physical reticence earlier. In both cases, communication is exclusively and intensely physical. This is indeed likely to be the case with a woman who can't speak the men's language, but in any event touch counts for a great deal in Hawks's films. One feels in *I Was a Male War Bride* how important a moment it is when Cary Grant rubs Ann Sheridan's back: below the mental antagonism the intuitive contact develops. Teal Eye's gift of a token to Jim is ambiguous: it means that she loves him, but, Zeb adds, 'like a brother'. Is she deliberately keeping him at a distance to get Boone, or is she being as forward as she can allow herself to be (remember her shame over the loss of her skirt, when the men rescued her from drowning)? And her attitude to Boone when he enters her tent—maidenly modesty or disappointment? I got the impression that the wrong man had come, and that she accepts Boone because it is the nearest she can get to Jim: she is submissive, more resigned than enthusiastic. Her farewell to Jim, with the sign that means 'Her heart is yours', shows deep sorrow.

The end of the film is emotionally very complex: very nearly tragic-ironic, but in fact triumphant. Boone's decision to return to Teal Eye (who was less valuable to him than the rifle with which he was asked to 'pay' for her) is made primarily in order to regain Jim's respect—not from love for the girl. Boone is chiefly conscious of Jim's scorn: their exchanged glances, in the incident of the payment for Teal Eye, and later on the boat and in the camp, are the film's moments of maximum intensity. Yet, the decision taken, Boone accepts it joyfully, with a sense of new-found freedom, returning to Teal Eye a happy man: it is an affirmative, not a tragic, ending. He has grown up. Crucial is the burning of the scalp, demonstrating his newly-gained independence of the

The Big Sky: payment for Teal Eye

elder-brother-figure. It is important that he *burns* it: if he were
thinking of Teal Eye he would have given it to her to bury. The
burning of the scalp marks less his acceptance of Indians than his
new freedom from his own obsessions. He casts off the immature
relationship for the mature one. His responsibility to Teal Eye was
casually incurred, and for confused and partly unconscious
motives; his growth to maturity is marked by his conscious
acceptance of it.

Come and Get It, Red River

Red River bears an even closer relationship to *Come and Get It*
than *The Big Sky* to *A Girl in Every Port*; here there is no doubt
of the superiority of the later film. A brief synopsis will make the
relationship clear: Ambitious young man loves girl but leaves her
to better himself. She dies. Time-gap. Man has reached middle
age and achieved material success, at the cost of inward hardening.
His son comes to oppose the rigidity of his course of action. Father

and son both fall in love with the dead girl's daughter. Tension between them mounts, but reliving the past through the girl helps the father to come to terms with himself. At the crisis, father and son begin to fight. The girl intervenes, and her presence is responsible for bringing the father to his senses, making him realise his love for his son, and leading him to accept the young people's marriage. In *Red River*, the 'son' is not a real son and the two women are unrelated; otherwise (and the differences are much less important than they sound) this synopsis would do for either film.

The relatedness is clear, its explanation obscure. *Come and Get It* is based on a novel by Edna Ferber, *Red River* on a story by Borden Chase. Hawks insists that *Come and Get It* (but not, apparently, *Red River*) is based on the story of his own grandfather. Was Edna Ferber's novel inspired by Hawks's grandfather? Does Hawks mean simply that he borrowed certain incidents (the saloon battle with the trays, for instance) from his grandfather's life, and tacked them on to the Ferber adaptation? I can offer, tentatively, one deduction. (*a*) Hawks left *Come and Get It* unfinished, after quarrelling with Samuel Goldwyn. It was completed by William Wyler, who used material Hawks had written for the ending (having found the original unsatisfactory). The last scenes *look* like Wyler, in their rather superficial, showy elegance: there is even a characteristic staircase shot. (*b*) Hawks, to judge from the Bogdanovich interview, was responsible for the decision not to have anyone killed at the end of *Red River*. (*c*) In terms of *events* (as opposed to direction), the closest parallel between the two films is in the endings, with father and son coming to blows and girl intervening. (*d*) (Rash?) deduction: this ending, on which the whole of *Red River* really depends, whether or not it has anything to do with Hawks's grandfather, is very personal to Hawks and his own conception.

Come and Get It has solid but conventional virtues. Before I learnt from Hawks that Wyler only shot 800 feet, I had been uncertain, apart from a few sequences, who had done what. The first part was clearly Hawks: the splendidly shot and cut

120

Come and Get It: candy-making

documentary on lumberjacking, the camaraderie which Barney Glasgow (Edward Arnold) loses when he gains financial success and social position, above all, the saloon fight in which Barney, the Swede (Walter Brennan), and Lotta (Frances Farmer, a vivacious and intelligent actress who plays mother in the first part and daughter in the second, equivalents of Coleen Gray and Joanne Dru in *Red River*) vanquish opposition by hurling tin trays. Later, there are only two scenes I felt like staking my life on: (1) Joel McCrea (Barney's son) visits Lotta Mark II in the house where his father has installed her (very Hawksian female-initiative/male-disadvantage opening, leading into a charming embryonic love scene where mutual sympathy develops through mutual candy-making); (2) Barney confronts his proletarian prospective son-in-law in the factory steam-room (very Hawksian self-respect reactions from the young man). The party at the end looked like Wyler (and presumably was). The rest of the film isn't particularly distinctive—one would never *guess* Hawks. Beside *Red River* it looks rather dull. The difference is of milieu. *Come and Get It*, after the first half hour, is the only non-comedy in Hawks's output set in American high society, and one senses the constraint: formal manners and sitting-rooms don't suit Hawks. Ill at ease, he chooses generally the safe, conventional way of doing things. The most striking thing about the film is that it exists. *Red River* had seemed something of an odd-film-out: deeply characteristic in many ways, quite untypical in others. Typically, his films don't greatly violate the classical unities; *Red River* covers a lot of time and ground, and the sense of gradual accumulation through time is all-important. This cumulative structure is anticipated in *Come and Get It* in considerable detail.

Rio Bravo has not a single shot that is visually beautiful; *Red River* is among the most striking of Westerns visually. The actual texture of life (the time of day, the atmosphere) and events has a thematic importance. The cattle-trek is conceived as a trial in which external pressures are exerted on tensions within the group and within the individuals who comprise it: we must be made aware of what it *feels* like to be in particular physical situations, cattle stampede, river-crossing, etc. It is worth singling out one shot: the burial of Dan Latimer (Harry Carey, jun.) after the cattle stampede, with the characters huddled round the grave in long-shot, the epitaph spoken by Dunson (John Wayne), 'We brought nothing into this world, and it's certain we can take nothing out', and a cloud shadow passing over the mountain in the background. In the foreground of the shot are dead steer and, on the drop-leaf of the chuck-wagon, some cans like those whose falling precipitated the stampede; the camera tracks back to reveal the whip Dunson will try to use on Bunk Kenneally. There is, clearly, more in the emotional effect than can be accounted for in terms of 'visual' beauty, but the shot remains visually beautiful in a way rare in Hawks. *Red River* is rooted in American history, in the establishing of a civilisation; it is traditional in a more narrowly defined sense than *Rio Bravo*, from which this 'historical' dimension is absent.

But it lacks the concentrated density of *Rio Bravo*, where, working in a studio with only a few actors, Hawks could encourage and organise a natural, organic development from the basic material. There are two weaknesses in the construction of *Red River* as we now have it: one, that the intriguing relationship between Montgomery Clift and John Ireland is so little developed, is partly due to distributors' cuts. The second, more important, is inherent in the conception of the film: Tess Millay (Joanne Dru) is introduced so late that the development of her relationships with the two men (Wayne and Clift) seems contrived.

Again, comparison with Ford is useful. During the river-crossing in *Wagon Master*, Ford gives us beautifully composed shots of wagons, water, and mountains, mostly in long-shot, with an effect of great formal beauty: the function of the long-shot seems more to make possible the compositional beauty than to give us an action entire (as in Hawks). On the soundtrack is a song, 'Wagons west are rolling', beginning with the line, 'A hundred years have come and gone since 1849'. Visually, we have the sense of looking at a landscape-painting; the song reminds us of the distance in time of the events we are watching. Nostalgia for a lost heroic past is strong here. The compositions in Hawks's film are equally beautiful but not nearly so 'composed'—less formal, more fluid. And we are put right in the middle of things: there are shots with the camera inside a wagon as it crosses the river, making the experience as present as possible. If Ford emphasises the pastness of the past, Hawks makes everything vividly present: there is very little nostalgia in *Red River*.

Well realised as they are, the 'historical' elements are not of *primary* importance to Hawks. The central character-conflict partly depends on them: the film traces the way in which Dunson's ruthlessness, necessary for survival in the primitive conditions in which the film begins, becomes obsolete as civilisation develops, so that the more liberal outlook of Matthew Garth (Montgomery Clift) gains him the men's allegiance as Dunson alienates it. But there isn't the same organic relation between the growth-of-civilisation theme and the more personal, psychological issues that one finds in the best Westerns of Anthony Mann. Borden Chase, who part wrote *Red River*, wrote most of Mann's best Westerns; and doubtless the 'historical' elements derive from him. The psychological tensions within the leading characters of *Where the River Bends* very accurately mirror the social conflict between civilised values and subversive elements. The emphasis at the end of *Red River* is on *personal* triumph rather than on the saving from starvation of the inhabitants of Abilene, on the fulfilment of a self-imposed task.

The ending of *Red River* has been much criticised. Everything hinges on why Dunson (John Wayne) doesn't shoot at Matthew Garth (Montgomery Clift) at the showdown. Our sympathy, unequivocally with Dunson at the beginning of the film, has been largely transferred to Matthew; the 'traditional' ending would have Wayne, the tragic hero of formidable moral stature but fatally flawed, killed (though not by Clift—we *are*, I think, sure that Matthew won't shoot), but achieving as he dies the clarity that enables him to judge himself and his actions, and leaving Matthew free for life. One feels that Hawks, in rejecting this ending, broke more than the rules of the traditional Western—he broke the rules of classical tragedy as well. None the less, if we attend properly to the film, we shall understand perfectly why Dunson doesn't try to shoot Matthew, though that understanding depends on our awareness of the whole structure, from the opening sequence to the moment of decision. Here lies the magnificence of the ending: there is no one easily formulable reason for the denouement but a whole complex of connected reasons. Even the word 'decision' needs modification: it is not a decision that Dunson consciously makes, but one that makes itself, with the whole film behind the making.

Dunson's farewell to Fen (Coleen Gray) as he leaves the wagon train, refusing to take her, is given strong visual emphasis partly through big close-ups (rare in the film as a whole), partly through the intensity of the actress (we, like Dunson, miss her), partly through the hauntingly beautiful compositions showing her, in long-shot, amid a vast and, apart from the wagon train, empty landscape. Already an obstinate man, he refuses Fen's pleas to take her; her 'You're wrong' (and her intense conviction convinces us that he is) will be taken up again and again in the film like an echo in Walter Brennan's 'You was wrong, Mr Dunson.' She is killed by Indians, and her death intensifies his obstinacy: to admit now that he was wrong would be to accept responsibility for it.

Fen was to join Dunson, they were to settle down and raise a family. On the morning after she dies, Dunson finds the boy Matthew, who becomes the son Fen would have borne him. He gave Fen a snake-bracelet which had been his mother's; we see it, after the fifteen-year time-gap, on Matthew's wrist. It represents for Dunson the continuity essential to his sense of purpose: he needs (since 'we brought nothing into this world, and it's certain we can take nothing out') something to pass on and somebody to pass it on to. The importance of son to father gets nothing like the same emphasis in *Come and Get It*. Dunson's herd develops from the mating of Dunson's bull and Matthew's cow. The cattle are marked with the Red River brand—the Red River being associated both with Fen's death and with the meeting with Matthew.

Red River: the whipping of Bunk Kenneally

The cattle-trek (on whose success the 'something to pass on' depends) is framed between two magnificent panning shots which mark two of the film's moments of greatest intensity: the pan over the waiting men and cattle before the dawn departure, conveying the enormousness of the enterprise and the initial solidarity of those taking part in it; and the pan over the cattle from right to left, steady and majestic, taking in at last the oncoming train and the railway line, at the moment of triumph and of Matthew's vindication. The trek imposes a series of tests on the characters and their relationships. Each incident either develops Dunson's ruthlessness or is provoked by it; at the same time the trek is a progressive initiation into manhood for Matthew. For the audience each development is a step in the transfer of allegiance from Dunson to Matthew. Dunson's ruthlessness at the outset of the film one accepted as a necessary (if dangerous) condition for survival and success. The film takes Dunson up to and beyond the limits of the

Red River: Dunson (John Wayne) and the 'quitters'

acceptability of this ruthlessness; in the course of the action we watch it hardening into insentience; his very humanity is in danger of becoming submerged. Similarly, we trace Matthew's development up to the point where we know that he must rebel against Dunson, his rebellion coinciding, as it were, with our own. The two young men principally involved in the cattle stampede—Bunk who provokes it, Dan who gets killed in it—are contrasting examples of immaturity to provide terms of comparison by which Matthew can be measured.

The river-crossing, culminating in the superb shots taken from inside the chuck-wagon as it plunges across, is a marvellous example of Hawks's ability to convey to the audience what it feels like to take part in an action. But its emotional force arises from context as much as from the sense of physical participation. It provides a point of rest, where Dunson's brutality and ruthlessness (he has already tried to horsewhip or kill Bunk, and shot three 'rebels') are balanced by our sense of his achievement, to which the ruthlessness was, up to a point, necessary. The sense of triumph at the crossing temporarily restores the solidarity by this time so gravely undermined; though this is partly offset by our anxiety as to what is to happen to the 'quitters' who disappeared the night before and whom Cherry (John Ireland) has been sent to bring back. The crossing is of the Red River of the title, where Dunson learnt of Fen's death, where he met Matthew, and where Dunson's bull met Matthew's cow: its associations have their indefinable role in the complex of reasons that makes Dunson, at the showdown, shoot at the dust and not his 'son'. The past is kept in our minds, and somewhere at the back of Dunson's: when he decides to cross, his remark ('This is as good a place as any') echoes word for word what he said when he stopped at the river to await the Indians who destroyed the wagon train and killed Fen.

We can now bring together the more concrete factors determining Dunson's decision not to kill Matthew. Dunson told the boy Matthew, at the start, that he couldn't have his initial on the brand until he had earned it; he 'earns it'—as Dunson finally recognises —by his rebellion, which marks his final assumption of manhood, the point at which loyalty to what he feels to be right takes precedence over loyalty to his 'father'. But Matthew proves his love for Dunson during the very act of rebellion, by saving his life: Clift's blazing eyes and trembling hand, when he almost kills Teeler for trying to kill Dunson, are tremendously expressive. The balance of betrayal and loyalty here takes us back to the 'trust' on which the relationship was founded: 'Never trust anyone until you know them' Dunson told Matthew when they first met, and a minute later gave the boy back his gun and turned his back. Events prove Matthew's decision right: the railroad *does* reach as far west as Abilene, the herd *does* get there, he has earned his initial on the brand. Yet we are kept aware that the achievement is a joint triumph. Matthew insists that the cheque for the cattle be made out to Dunson. As Dunson approaches Abilene, ostensibly to kill Matthew, a series of emotionally very powerful shots show him moving through the cattle massed in and around the town—*his* cattle, there because of *his* initial impetus. We see him, to enter the town, cross the railway line: Hawks, refusing to be explicit about the *dénouement* in the dialogue, keeps us constantly aware visually of the emotional factors that count in it.

But none of these *would* count were it not for the presence of Tess. Only by reliving—if by proxy—the original experience with Fen can Dunson be released from the pattern of inflexible obstinacy that his behaviour repeats: Matthew, obstinately, has left Tess behind until things are safe, despite her protests, and Dunson is forced to recognise his son's likeness to him. (The Dunson-Tess dialogue makes the parallels between Tess and Fen too explicit: one feels the rush to communicate a lot in a short time.) When Dunson meets Tess, she is wearing the snake-bracelet (given her by Matthew) which Dunson once put on Fen. She and Matthew are in love. Only Dunson's fixed ruthlessness obstructs the fulfilment of his deepest need—the establishment of continuity. Why is Tess's intervention in the final fight so moving and so right? Because the whole emotional weight of the film is behind it, Fen, her death, and its importance to Dunson being as significantly present here in memory and association as Tess herself in the flesh. The ending carries a great sense of fulfilment. *Red River* may lack the density of organisation of *Rio Bravo*, but it is by no means the rambling and episodic work it may appear to the casual observer.

6: The Instinctive Consciousness

Hatari! (1962), *Man's Favourite Sport?* (1964), *Red Line 7000* (1965)

Hatari!

Often in Hawks strong superficial resemblances between films conceal deeper differences. If time and repeated viewings have confirmed *Hatari!*'s inferiority to *Rio Bravo*—it isn't the film one would send anyone to to convince him of Hawks's greatness—they have also revealed a more interesting film than was at first apparent.

In so far as it repeats earlier films *Hatari!* is indeed markedly inferior. Fairly typical is the almost literal transplanting of the piano-playing scene from *Only Angels Have Wings*: the man, trying to play a tune, repeatedly hits a wrong note; the girl corrects him a few times then takes over; he says to her, 'You'd better be good'; she is. The incident in the original had a particular context that gave it terrific tension: it followed the death of Joe, and marked Bonnie's acceptance of the fliers' world—beneath the action one sensed layers of emotional conflict. In *Hatari!* the scene marks Dallas's acceptance into the hunters' circle, and supplies another charming example (Dallas at the piano, Pockets on the harmonica) of intuitive communication-through-music, confirming the contact between the two characters that developed in the preceding scene; but one feels it has become primarily a party-piece, given for itself. This sufficiently defines the tone of the film, although it leaves much to be said about its content. There is something of the air of an informal party, of long duration, at which one is never bored, but at which one cannot fight down a sense that the

Hatari!: capture of the rhinoceros

relaxed atmosphere is preventing all these obviously pleasant and entertaining people from revealing their deeper potentialities. There is insufficient tension either within or between the characters to sustain any deep interest in the relationships; we don't feel it as a matter of really pressing importance when Dallas (Elsa Martinelli) leaves without marrying Sean (John Wayne)—we just feel it is rather a pity, and are quite pleased when she is recaptured. Our degree of involvement in all this seems accurately to reflect Hawks's. The 'danger' of the title is too exclusively physical.

There are the hunting sequences, surely the most beautiful and exhilarating ever filmed. The camera, in the moving truck, puts us in the middle of it all; and we like the characters well enough for involvement in the danger and exhilaration to be more than merely technical. The actors did it all themselves, and we see this. Where almost any other director would give us the star pulling on one end of the rope, then cut to the rhinoceros pulling on the (alleged) other end, Hawks gives us Wayne and rhinoceros in the

A Song is Born: the Polynesian mating-dance

same shot. No back-projection, no stand-ins. The sense of reality adds to the beauty of many characteristic images of men carrying out with full mastery the difficult and dangerous tasks they have undertaken, in a context of great exposed plains and vast distances.

But to see in *Hatari!* only amiable repetition of things done better, spiced with brilliant action sequences, is to miss all that is new in the film, and all that is most important. Its relationship to the other adventure films is obvious; that to the comedies is more fundamental. Hawks has always been fascinated by the relationship between sophisticated modern life and primitive life, whether in savages or animals. In *Scarface* the gangsters are implicitly compared to savages, with Tony Camonte introduced as an ape-like shadow on a wall. There are the animals in *Bringing up Baby*, the redskin game in *Monkey Business*. There is also a striking incident in *A Song is Born*, not imported from *Ball of Fire*, where timid, super-civilised Professor Frisbee (Danny Kaye) teaches the repressed spinster benefactor Miss Totten (Mary Field) a

Polynesian mating chant and dance, and under its influence they begin to throw off all inhibitions. The relationship between humans and animals or sophisticated Westerners and savages, constitutes *Hatari!*'s principle of composition. In the earlier films one was chiefly aware of dislocation—of the rational and the instinctive, the civilised and the primitive, hopelessly at war. In *Hatari!* one finds serenity and harmony. In the perfect Hawksian society that the hunters' world embodies, all the tensions between the attraction to the primitive-instinctive and the need for conscious control and mastery that we have found so often in Hawks's work are resolved.

The hunters of *Hatari!* are in continual physical contact with animals: they hunt them for zoos, not to kill. Catching involves handling—Sean clutches a giraffe's legs, others handle zebra and wildebeeste. Chips (Gérard Blain) and Brandy (Michèle Girardon) water the hyena with a hose, Dallas washes her baby elephants. Hundreds of monkeys are caught and handled; a tame cheetah (Sonia) moves freely among the humans; even Pockets (Red Buttons), who is scared of animals, tries to milk a goat (which turns out to be a ram). Certain scenes call to mind (not very favourably for the film) D. H. Lawrence's characteristic use of animals to suggest the intuitive consciousness (mare and rabbit in *Women in Love*, mole in *Second Best*, the snake in the poem *Snake*, etc.): Chips and Brandy's handling of the hyena, playful and relaxed, suggests their attitude to their relationship, to their animal instincts.

The sense of easy-going intimacy with the animal kingdom is confirmed by the charming parallels and contrasts between human beings and animals. During the giraffe hunt, the inexperienced Dallas (not yet fully initiated into the hunters' society) falls helplessly around in the bumpy truck in which she has insisted on standing to take pictures, and the editing contrasts her ungainly lurching and sprawling with the lithe, loping grace of the giraffes. Her pursuit of Sean neatly reverses his usual role of hunter. When the orphaned baby elephant is found, Dallas immediately takes the place of its mother, defending it with her life; she solves the problem of feeding it by thinking in terms of a human baby; she

becomes known to the natives as 'Mama Tembo', or elephant-mother. From then on she is constantly associated with the elephant, and the other two babies that join it, as a mother-figure. Kurt (Hardy Kruger) and Chips, both attracted to Brandy, are like young bucks (Sean makes the comparison explicitly, but we have already watched them squaring up to one another like rival stags in the mating season). They refer to Brandy as 'our girl', go every-where together with her (partly because they don't trust each other, partly because they like each other; they seem quite happy to share her just as, at the end of the film, they are planning to visit a girl Chips knows in Paris: 'We go halves'); the sequence establishing this is followed by the escape and recapture of the ostriches, the male being caught and penned whereupon the females both come running, neatly reversing the human relation-ship. Pockets's fear and distrust of animals is reflected in his difficulty in making contact with Brandy and his inability to realise that she loves him. Pockets, watching Dallas wash her 'babies', says to Sean, 'She could even do it to me.' He captures hundreds of monkeys without daring to look, and wins Brandy without realising it. At the end of the film, Dallas is 'hunted' through the town by the men converging in two vehicles, exactly as we have watched animals hunted on the plains; the reversal-pattern is completed by having the baby elephants converge on her in the hotel lobby, like truck and jeep converging on the rhinoceros in the film's opening and climactic hunts. The film is pervaded by an unconstrained naturalness, arising from the easy acceptance of man's relatedness to the animals, from the reconciliation of animal instinct and human consciousness. The society of *Monkey Business*, built on the suppression of the instincts, bears a significant negative relationship to the ideal Hawksian society of the hunters.

One curious and striking scene deserves separate comment: that in which Dallas takes her baby elephants for a wash and romp in a pool away from camp, and is menaced by full-grown wild elephants. Up to the appearance of the wild elephants, the sequence is another example, beautiful and funny, of the animal/human correspon-dences: Sean, unknown to Dallas, follows at a distance with his gun,

Hatari!: Brandy, Chips and the hyena

Hatari!: the initiation of Dallas

and the scene becomes a family outing with mother romping with the kids while the father-protector (like a male animal) stands guard. (Compare the delightful domestic scene with which the film ends, where Dallas's three 'babies' clamber on to and demolish the bridal bed.) Where the scene adds to this ubiquitous leitmotif of human/animal intercourse is in the sudden awareness of danger—of *things beyond*, unassimilable into the general harmony: beyond the harmonising control of the consciousness. The progression here from tame baby elephants to dangerous wild adults interestingly parallels the progression from tame 'Baby' to wild leopard in *Bringing up Baby.*

Apart from the animals, there are the savages. Especially interesting is Dallas's tribal initiation. Carried off by the Warusha villagers, blackened and bangled in preparation for the ceremony so that she is barely recognisable, she participates in the dance grudgingly, yet with an implicit admission of the appropriateness of doing so, an acknowledgement of the continuity between the primitive and the civilised. The scene bears a most suggestive and complex relationship to the redskin game in *Monkey Business*. It is followed by the scene where Sean visits Dallas in her bedroom, where the blacking has been replaced by an even thicker application of cold cream to suggest a parallel between primitive and 'civilised' ritual adornments. He can now take the initiative and kiss her—through the cream—because she is at last at a disadvantage?—because she 'was good today'? He treats her with a charming combination of respect and ironic humour that reflects Hawks's attitude. She has lived through the day's experiences and their implications and remained—not without a certain sophisticated resentment—mistress of herself.

The characters' easy traffic with the instinctive and the primitive is balanced by their equally easy commerce with the rational, conscious side of man's nature and the inventions and implements that are its products. Trucks, jeeps, radio, even rockets, are assimilated into the general harmony. Hawks's fondness for showing people's intuitive sympathy with each other expressed through singing together receives one of its most striking expressions in the group performance of 'Whisky leave me alone' over the intercommunications system between truck and jeep on the joyous ride home from the hospital. The scene anticipates the juxtaposition in *Red Line 7000* of lives lived with extreme instinctive spontaneity and all the supposedly dehumanising paraphernalia of our civilisation, the world of racing-cars and transistors. *Hatari!* is a celebration of man's empirical synthesising intelligence—his ability, in ideal circumstances, to use and harmonise everything that is there, to be master of himself and his environment without destroying or suppressing any essential part of himself. Its principle of harmony, assimilation, and balance sets off very clearly the imbalances Hawks deals with in *Monkey Business* and *The Thing*.

All of which explains why *Hatari!* is such a pleasing and enjoyable film. It must be admitted that, thematically as in narrative, it all hangs together rather loosely, without that sense of pressing inner necessity that makes us feel in the presence of a masterpiece. It is a film that makes one wish, as *Rio Bravo* doesn't, that Hawks were, not perhaps a more conscious artist, but more consciously an artist: in *Hatari!* he has been content to be a relaxed entertainer, and the richness of the material leaves one feeling somewhat dissatisfied that more wasn't done with it—a more rigorous following-through and realising of its implications. If the functions of the animals in *Hatari!* occasionally calls to mind the use of animals by Lawrence, Hawks (not even here, far less in *Bringing up Baby*!) shows little of Lawrence's intense sensitive response to animals or to the human qualities Lawrence uses them to represent, and, given *Hatari!*'s theme, this constitutes a radical limiting criticism. *Bringing up Baby* tended (through the whole conception of Hepburn's part, and her relationship to the leopard) to trivialise animal nature; *Hatari!* doesn't exactly trivialise it, but neither does it invest it with the vividness, the energy and sensitivity that Lawrence communicates.

Man's Favourite Sport?

Man's Favourite Sport? needs brief notice here because of its relationship to the films that flank it. It is to the earlier comedies what *Hatari!* is to the adventure films: there are obvious, and inferior, reminiscences, and less obvious novelties, but the degree of success is much less. If the word that sprang to mind for *Hatari!* was 'relaxed', the word for its successor is 'tired'. The very slow tempo draws attention to the weakness of much of the material. One guesses that Hawks's relationship with his actors was not entirely satisfactory. Rock Hudson's performance is somewhat laborious, and it was cruel to make him repeat the night-club scene from *Bringing up Baby* which Cary Grant brought off with such panache; Paula Prentiss is—as always—very good, but at times one has the feeling that Hawks is imposing a characterisation on her instead of working *with* her. Parts of the film seem in a limiting way old-fashioned: situations in which a woman can't be told that another woman has (quite innocently) spent the night in her fiancé's rooms would be more at home in thirties comedy.

The film has its defenders. What would they have made of it

had they seen it without knowing it was by Hawks? They would have recognised the Hawks influence immediately, of course; but wouldn't they have dismissed the film as an inferior imitation? The high value they place on it arises from its clear thematic relationship to Hawks's other work: there is an understandable but unhelpful tendency to confuse this with artistic achievement.

The basic conception is characteristic: a hero from a safe, civilised, and limited environment where his responsibilities exist purely on a mental-theoretical level (in fact, a fishing equipment salesman, in terms of book-learning the complete expert, who has never actually fished), is plunged into an environment where he must act practically, instinctively, and physically (a fishing tournament). The most interesting feature of the film (in relation to Hawks's past work) is the character's development. The crucial scene in the film is the public confession, where he achieves honesty with his acquaintances and with himself. The decision to confess marks a development more decisive than any undergone by the heroes of Hawks's previous comedies; as in *Hatari!* (though here to a lesser extent) the relaxation is partly compensated for by a new mellowness and serenity. If at the end of the film the hero is still (now literally) drifting, it is from choice, not mere misadventure.

Hatari!, *Man's Favourite Sport?*, and *Red Line 7000* can be seen as a loose trilogy. All three are constructed on parallels between man's efforts to master something dangerous, recalcitrant and non-human (rhinoceroses, fish, racing-cars) and his efforts to cope with his own life and his relationships with women. Beyond this, all three are concerned (on whatever level of conscious or subconscious intention) with the relationship between the conscious and the instinctive. In this 'trilogy' *Man's Favourite Sport?* has an importance beyond its intrinsic merits: it represents an inversion of the unifying theme, showing a man hopelessly at odds with both fish (sexual symbolism?) and women, unable to come to terms with his instinctive-physical side. In the light of this the ending (man and woman happily adrift together on the water) could be taken as representing his acceptance of himself. The parallels between women and fish pervade the film much as the humans/animals comparisons pervade *Hatari!* but the organisation is looser still, the incidental invention (one or two excellent scenes apart) uninspired. It looked as if Hawks would from now on rest content amiably to repeat himself. *Red Line 7000* proved this assumption quite false.

Red Line 7000

Red Line 7000 is perhaps, in Britain at least, the most under-estimated film of the sixties. The critics more or less ignored it, the public (who hadn't heard of any of the actors) kept away. Hawks himself dislikes it: it is difficult to see why. It is an intensely personal film, based on an original Hawks story and showing in its realisation every mark of close involvement; Hawks's statement that he lost interest in it is belied by every shot. It has precisely what its two immediate predecessors lacked: the degree of creative intensity that prompts a consistent exactness of touch, a tautness and economy and sense of relevance in the total organisation. With its coherence goes a youthful vitality not entirely attributable to the (on the whole) admirably energetic and responsive young cast (though they doubtless proved an important stimulus). The tension and economy in the whole cinematic complex—dialogue, acting, use of camera, editing—are untypical of late Hawks, though every sequence is unmistakably Hawksian. In any work of art one's response to local realisation is a more reliable guide to evaluation than a generalised sense of what the work is about. Examine any sequence of *Red Line 7000*, and you will find an unfailing rightness in the direction, corresponding to Hawks's sense of what is important in the action at any given moment. Look, particularly, at the sequences where the Mike/Gaby relationship is worked out; or at (a model of economical exposition) the early scenes between Laura Devon and John Robert Crawford. Indeed, the economy throughout the film is such that one feels Hawks was trying to see how much he could leave out—or, alternatively, how much he could pack in; seldom in a film can so much ground have been covered in so short a time.

Red Line 7000: Ned and Julie

With this rediscovered creative intensity one finds, significantly, new thematic developments. The film offers new departures for Hawks in all its major relationships. The scene introducing Ned Arp (John Robert Crawford) and Julie Kazarian (Laura Devon) recalls (while remaining fresh and alive) many instant-sex-antagonism scenes in previous Hawks films; only here the man manages to hold his own, and it is he, not the girl, who is sexually experienced. Both Dan McCall (James Ward) and Mike Marsh (James Caan) relate interestingly to the John Wayne characters in *Rio Bravo* and *Hatari!*, but in quite different ways. McCall has the same kind of mastery of himself and his profession (consequently the same ability to help the fallible) as Chance and Sean. But, with Dan, the mastery extends to his relationships with women. The scene in which he visits Holly MacGregor (Gail Hire) in the back room of Lindy's club and forces her to confront her perverse and obstructive superstition, recalls at once—in the stronger character's rigorously unsentimental treatment of the

weaker—Wayne's handling of Dean Martin in *Rio Bravo*; only here it is a woman on the receiving end. (This whole scene—along with several other things—was hacked out of the film by the British distributors for its general release in this country. Mike Marsh has the Hawks hero's characteristic difficulties with women, but here they are presented explicitly as neurotic in origin (a point one couldn't help inferring in the Wayne films, for all Hawks's dexterity in evading it). As such, they cease to be funny and become dangerous. McCall and Marsh represent a separating out of the components of previous Hawks heroes; the main climax of the film is precipitated when they come into direct conflict, so that one tries to destroy the other. Further, the Wildcat Jones of Holly MacGregor's song carries a strong suggestion of self-parody (intensified by the bizarre accompaniment of what has been described as 'a quartet of female dwarfs').

The opening conversation between Mike Marsh and Jim Loomis suggests a parallel between success in racing and success in personal relationships: Jim takes a question about the former as referring to the latter. The parallel pervades the film, determining its structure, becoming explicit (though never insistently so) at certain points in the dialogue (e.g. Pat Kazarian to Ned Arp: '. . . there's not a car you can't handle, no girl you can't spoil'; or the connection Mike makes, in his apology to Dan McCall for trying to kill him, between being through with racing and losing Gaby); but there is no schematic sub-Freudian collocation of handling cars and handling women. Perhaps the best example of all—it also suggests the link with *Hatari!*—arises from Gaby's comparison of controlling a racing-car to lion-taming. Later she admits that the fascination she feels for Mike is due to his strangeness. The implied common factor, the desire to control something unpredictable and potentially dangerous, is central both to Gaby's psychology and to the theme of the film. Motor-racing, like wild-animal-catching, demands a full development of the intuitive consciousness, of the ability to *think instinctively*. Reason ratifies instinct. One senses that this is how Hawks makes his films, with their combination of spontaneity and satisfyingly organic

Red Line 7000: Dan and Holly

construction: instinct, prompted by the pressures of the moment, of the actual circumstances in which he is involved, tells him what to do, then reason endorses, controls, modifies, elaborates. In *Red Line 7000* this relationship between instinct and empirical intelligence is the foundation of the behaviour of most of the characters most of the time, out of cars as well as in. The men have a highly developed instinctive awareness and the readiness to put into action unhesitatingly whatever it indicates, acquired through their professional efficiency. But the same is true of the women, whose connection with racing, though close, is necessarily indirect. Julie, younger sister of the team manager Pat Kazarian, treated by him in some respects like a younger brother ('You're talking like a girl'), and an expert motor-cyclist, knows at once that Ned Arp will be worth trying as a driver, and this is inseparable from her instantaneous attraction to him as a man; Gaby (Marianna Hill), who adores racing, has been the mistress of a champion, and wants to drive a racing-car herself, knows at once that she wants Mike Marsh and is prompt at improvising the means of meeting him. All three of the film's main relationships begin with an almost instantaneous attraction, and the development of each gets its impetus from the use by one or both partners of an empirical intelligence that both creates and seizes opportunities. The parallel with racing is never far below the surface of the film: 'KEEP BRAIN in GEAR at ALL TIMES' (the slogan above the dashboard in the opening, pre-credit, shot) can well stand as its motto.

Essential to success in racing is flexibility. Each of the three relationships contains a flaw, and in each case the flaw arises from some rigidity that interferes with moral or emotional flexibility, frustrates the free working of instinct and empirical intelligence. A diagrammatically simple (but unforced and unobtrusive) statement of the progress of the film is made through two races: one is in the middle of the film (where all three relationships are approaching crises), in which all three men have breakdowns or collisions. Even here, there is no schematic parallel between problem and breakdown though one might find symbolism in Mike's near-asphyxiation—his neurotic sexual attitude is interfering in his relationship with Gaby. In the other race, at the end (when the basic problems in the relationships have been resolved), all three circumvent the difficulties they encounter on the track. With Ned Arp the rigidity is his obsession with money and success, combined with his attitude to women which is a matter of general knowledge and particular ignorance. He has had plenty of experience with girls—where he comes from, they're the only alternative to watching TV in the evenings—but to him they are all much the same, or sorted into rigid categories as if they were objects ('tall and short, sexy or not sexy. . . .'). The love scene—it consists of one long static take, yet is intensely cinematic—in which Julie asks him how he knows when girls are sexy (longing to be told that *she* is) derives its poignancy from the contrast between her openness, transparency, and vulnerability and Ned's stolid lack of response to her as an individual. In Holly MacGregor we see how an instinctive, irrational reaction has set in an attitude which her reason can neither correct nor modify: three men in love with her have died, therefore she brings bad luck, the same will happen to the next. More is involved here than superstition. Lindy (Charlene Holt) tells Holly that she uses her sense of being the cause of men's deaths to give herself a feeling of her own importance, and other aspects of Holly's behaviour confirm this hint of perverse pride: her treatment of Dan, for example, when, after their meeting, he invites her in for a drink. It is with Mike, however, that Hawks gives us the clearest statement of a positive instinctive impulse being impaired and frustrated by an inflexible habitual attitude. He sees Gaby dancing with a controlled and flexible abandon that marvellously expresses her character, is instantaneously drawn to her, then, learning she is Dan's girl, turns away in recoil to get a drink. We assume he is annoyed because she is already attached; later, Mike reveals a neurotic revulsion at the idea of having a woman who has been another man's—or quite simply a girl who isn't a virgin.

The Mike/Gaby relationship and this tension between instinct and neurosis is developed in one of the film's most beautiful sequences. Unable to make contact in conversation, they achieve

an intuitive-sympathetic communication through common involvement in two shared pleasures: first, singing together to music over the car radio, then driving. Gaby drives round the race-track in the dark under Mike's supervision, the two acting almost as the eyes, mind, and physical-instinctive reactions of a single being. The spectator shares the sensation that unites them, the sense of togetherness in danger, communicated by movement and editing. Then, the drive over, Gaby innocently mentions Dan, and Mike is instantly alienated.

Of the characters in *Red Line 7000* Dan McCall—he is a champion driver—most nearly approaches the Hawksian ideal, being unhampered by inner tensions, consequently mature and flexible in his attitudes and free to help others. (It is a pity that the actor lacks the necessary authority for the part—he is the one weak link in the chain of unknown or relatively new players.) Dan has brought Gaby over from France: when they realise that their affair has failed to develop into deep love, they break it off quite simply, accepting the fact as a fact, without analysis of causes, but retaining mutual respect and friendship. Shortly after the scene in which the break is achieved, not without sorrow but with dignity and adult sense, we get Mike's hostile comment: 'A guy brings a girl three thousand miles and then he drops her.' The remark betrays the rigid morality that associates with neurosis. His horror of having a girl someone else has touched is unobtrusively placed when Gaby asks Dan how his relationship with Holly is progressing. He tells her it's going well, she asks him to tell Holly how glad she is, and he says, '*You* tell her—she'd like it.' Such comparisons, arising from the complex structure of the film, define its standards of adult behaviour.

Hawks's characters are seldom introspective; their empirical intelligence is directed outwards towards the circumstances in which they are involved. Inner disturbances tend to be resolved through experience-therapy rather than self-analysis. One of the best examples of this is Dunson in *Red River* (from his meeting with Tess Millay). Another, where the experience is less direct in psycho-analytic relevance yet convincingly cathartic in its violence,

Red Line 7000: Gaby and Mike

is Mike's attempted murder of Dan. By following through the uncontrollable impulses arising from his neuroses, Mike is forced into an awareness he could not otherwise have achieved. This is the focal point of the film, resolving in one instant two of the three relationship problems. The race sequence derives its intensity not only from the direct physical impact—staggering as this is—and its concentrated economy (it is scarcely above a minute in duration), but also from its context. Not just Dan's life is at stake, but the lives of three other people. *Red Line 7000* involves the spectator more intensely than *Hatari!*, because the relationships it presents matter so much more than those in the earlier film.

Logically, the resolution should be tragic: Dan killed, the lives of Holly (reconfirmed in her morbid superstition), Mike, and Gaby in ruins. That it isn't depends on sheer chance. Far from being a weakness, this recognition of the limitations of man's mastery over circumstances is the film's final strength. In *Rio Bravo* when Dean Martin pours the whisky back into the bottle 'without spilling a drop', he is able to do so, we can say, because of his own basic strength, and because it has been revived and developed through his relationship with Chance; but all this would have gone for nothing if the 'Alamo' music hadn't started up at the precise second. Similarly, Mike and Holly are cured because they have progressed, through the relationships with partners who are healthy, 'open', and flexible, to the point at which cure is possible; but whether there is cure or irremediable disaster depends finally on Dan's surviving the crash. The survival is near-miraculous: the images tell us that, unlike Wildcat Jones, the comic-strip superman of Holly's song (whom she associates with Dan as she sings it—the song ironically anticipates the film's climax), Dan could have done little to affect the outcome of the crash. This is not a complacency-inducing Happy End: the spectator, along with the characters, is left with too great a sense of precariousness. The film ends with a race in which all three heroes overcome the difficulties they encounter; but the last shot is of a blazing car which the women, startled, leap to their feet to see. It isn't the car of one of the characters we know, but the image fixes in our minds the sense that it might have been any of them . . . and may be, in the next race.

The main *dénouement* leaves the Ned/Julie relationship still to be resolved: one's first reaction is a feeling of anti-climax, which seems confirmed by the cursory resolution that follows. But the unsatisfactoriness is dramatically valid: the failure is in the relationship, not the film. The fact that the Ned/Julie relationship is so little integrated in the main action is not really the structural fault it at first appears. The other two relationships are parallel: in both, a strong, mature partner (Dan, Gaby) helps someone whose development has been arrested (Holly, Mike); the threads of plot continually interweave. The Ned/Julie relationship offers a contrast, and Hawks keeps it separate. Here, both partners are immature; Ned's failure to see Julie as she is provokes a correspondingly inflexible attitude (tenacious devotion and self-sacrifice) in her, held in defiance of the discernible facts and so the reverse of empirical (see the scene where she comes to ask Lindy for a job). In the hospital scene we see a tentative compromise achieved, but no more. Where the other relationships are resolved, this is patched up. The resolution of the Mike/Gaby relationship is set in the pouring rain—there is release and purification. The Ned/Julie compromise is reached in a sombre hospital room with rain pouring down outside: the atmosphere is heavy and oppressive, and any suggestion of release in the action is qualified by Ned's immediate inflexible insistence (with Julie in his arms) on his need to continue driving—his obsession with fame and money remains largely untouched. The film's last shots of him, driving with a hook instead of a left hand, with evident strain and handicap, offer a good image (given the constant racing/relationships comparison) of how his life will be lived.

One particularly interesting feature of *Red Line 7000* is the world in which it is set. It is, characteristically, a world apart, yet it bears a remarkably close relation to certain of the more 'advanced' aspects of modern civilisation. The action of the film is played out against a background of machines, transistor radios, pop music, and brand names: the sense of impermanence characteristic of the adventure films (for instance, *Only Angels Have Wings*) is here linked to the impermanence about us. Only Hawks, perhaps, among great artists—with his 'primitive' qualities, and his lack of interest in tradition—could face that impermanence in so positive a spirit of acceptance; that he can do so suggests both his strength and his limitations. After the slightly old-fashioned quality of *Man's Favourite Sport?*, *Red Line 7000* comes across as an intensely modern film: its principle of precariousness and impermanence relates right back to *Only Angels Have Wings*, yet at the same time is very much of the sixties. Much of the film's excitement derives from its surprising juxtaposition of mechanised civilisation and intense instinctive vitality—the vitality, as in *Only Angels Have Wings*, deriving partly from the sense of impermanence, and its resultant tension and exhilaration.

In dealing thus with the groundwork of *Red Line 7000*, one is not claiming any profundity for the extractable moral-metaphysical ideas, which are quite simple and straightforward, though never stupid or trivial. Hawks is an artist, not a 'thinker'; the fact that nothing in *Red Line 7000* is incompatible with the idea that the moral-metaphysical basis was quite unconscious is simply the measure of how completely he *is* an artist. All the 'meaning' of the film is implicit in the action, never imposed on it. There is no obtrusive symbolism, the camera is at no point used to force a point of view on the spectator. Hawks is perhaps too completely an artist for many critics to see that he is one at all: they need some symbols and 'striking' camera-angles and overt moral points flourished at them before they think they're seeing anything significant. The greatness of Hawks's films lies not in the extractable moral viewpoint itself, but in the intensity with which it is felt and realised in concrete terms.

The History of *Red Line 7000* in Britain

Red Line 7000 opened in London with a minimum of advance publicity and ran for a fortnight at the Plaza, Piccadilly Circus, playing to almost deserted houses. It was then taken off and shelved for some months, at the end of which time it was put out on release, severely mutilated, in a double bill with Cornel Wilde's *The Naked Prey*. As it seems likely that no complete prints now exist in Britain it seems worth tabulating this act of vandalism in detail.

The cuts are as follows:

1. The introduction of Holly MacGregor. The men go from the car park to Mike's flat, and find the door open and pop music blaring forth; they look at each other with expressions of distaste (Jim's funeral is just over), then go in to find Holly unconscious on the bed, either drunk or in a state of emotional exhaustion or both.

2. The trial of Ned Arp as a driver: the fact that he has been given an imperfect car was originally established *before* the test. As the sequence now stands, most of the suspense is destroyed.

3. The first meeting of Mike and Gaby. In the film as it stands there is a mysterious reference to this in the scene where they now appear to be meeting for the first time.

4. Most of the charming scene where Dan invites Holly in for a drink and she and Gaby speak French together (which he can't understand). The ease with which relationships between the three develop is very important.

5. The whole scene of the showdown between Holly and Dan in the shaded back room of Lindy's club. The later scene where Dan visits Holly when she is painting now looks absurdly abrupt and unmotivated; the scene is among the most important—and most dramatic—in the film.

6. The prelude to Gaby's and Mike's nocturnal drive, where they sit in Mike's car singing together to the car radio.

7. The whole scene of Pat Kazarian's visit to Ned the morning after it becomes clear that Ned has abandoned Julie. Pat denounces him bitterly; Ned remains defiant.

8. Julie's visit to the club to ask Lindy and Holly for a job. Very important for the development of Julie's character.

7: Down the Valley of the Shadow

El Dorado (1966)

El Dorado is, at the moment, the most difficult of Hawks's films to come to terms with. Its relationship to *Rio Bravo* poses a number of difficulties, and commonly provokes two reactions: the critic who doesn't rate Hawks particularly high but likes *Rio Bravo* well enough (it is a difficult film to dislike), sees the similarities and decides that the new film is more or less the same and just as good; the critic whose admiration for Hawks and especially for *Rio Bravo* is intense, sees the similarities and writes *El Dorado* off as an artistic disaster. Both views are, I now feel, quite wrong, though the second was an early reaction of my own.

El Dorado is not as great a film as *Rio Bravo*; indeed, considered in isolation from the rest of Hawks's work (an almost impossible thing to do), it is not a *great* film at all. The difficulty for the critic arises not only from the fact that the superficial resemblances to *Rio Bravo*, though so close, are misleading; there is also the fact that, although everything important in *El Dorado* is new, it is in many ways dependent on the earlier film for its significance. It is precisely our *awareness* of its differences from *Rio Bravo* that matters.

That it is not entirely satisfying considered as a self-sufficient entity is in various ways confirmed if we place it beside *Rio Bravo*: its relatively loose, and in some respects contrived, organisation becomes immediately apparent in relation to its great forerunner's tightness and naturalness. *Rio Bravo* grows organically out of

Dude's alcoholism; the alcoholism of J. P. Harrah (Robert Mitchum) is brought in arbitrarily because Hawks lost faith in the script he started with and decided to do *Rio Bravo* again. One can only guess at the reasons for this decision. Both Hawks's own description of the original script (taken from Harry Brown's novel *The Stars in their Courses*) as Greek tragedy, and the part of it that survives in the finished film (the episode of the boy's suicide) suggest that he was here toying with the idea of doing something (for him) completely new. One doesn't know to what extent commercial considerations influenced him, but the fact that both *Man's Favourite Sport?* and *Red Line 7000* (the latter of which, at least, broke new ground for Hawks) did badly at the box-office, whereas *Rio Bravo* has proved among his most popular films, may be significant. An artist, however firmly established, working in a commercial medium, can only allow himself a limited number of box-office disasters before it becomes difficult to find backing; and, beyond that, there is the popular artist's understandable desire to please his audiences and go on pleasing them. At the same time, that complete unpretentiousness which is Hawks's greatest strength and greatest limitation—which gives his films their unselfconscious spontaneity, and prevents him from thinking of them in ways that go beyond the principle of 'having fun'—may have acted as an automatic veto. A Greek tragedy directed by Howard Hawks sounds a rather absurd contradiction in terms; yet the episode of the suicide and its aftermath is so poignant in its bareness and its stoical grief that one can't help regretting the film Hawks didn't make, and wondering what it might have been.

One can start from certain obvious ways in which *El Dorado*, even at points of greatest similarity, differs from *Rio Bravo*: it pushes to conspicuous extremes two features that in the earlier film are so perfectly integrated in the tone that one is hardly aware of them as isolatable characteristics: humour and violence. On the one hand, there is a marked broadening of the comedy: things like the 'cure' for Mitchum's alcoholism, and James Caan's imitation of a Chinaman, are more farcical and more grotesque than anything in *Rio Bravo*. On the other hand, the violence is carried much

El Dorado: the Sheriff in the tub

further than in the earlier film. At times, this tendency to carry things to excess is attributable to Hawks's awareness that he is repeating himself and his consequent concern to elaborate on familiar incidents in case they go dead on him: consider, for example, what becomes in *El Dorado* of the incidents in *Rio Bravo* where Wayne strikes a lying enemy in the face with a gun, and where Dean Martin, after much pressure has been brought to bear on him, has a bath.

There is also in *El Dorado* a new, and very insistent, emphasis on pain: Luke Macdonald, shot in the stomach, commits suicide because he can't bear the pain; Joey Macdonald (Michele Carey) shoots Cole Thornton (Wayne) in the side, the bullet lodges up against his spine, and he is periodically doubled up in agony and semi-paralysed; Harrah strikes Bart Jason hard across the face with a gun-barrel; Thornton, forcing a gunman out through a door to face an ambush meant for *him*, shoots him first in the shoulder, then in the leg; Nelse Macleod (Christopher George) is shot several times by Thornton before he dies. In all these instances, pain is not merely implicit in the action, it is emphasised by the way it is presented. The humour and the pain are on the whole quite separate (the exceptions mainly involve the use of James Caan's shotgun); there is nothing in *El Dorado* like the scene of the finger-amputation in *The Big Sky*. There, a potentially painful scene was played as riotous farce, with Kirk Douglas and his friends crawling round the camp-fire to search for the discarded bit of finger in accordance with the old Indian (or Polynesian—*Tiger Shark*—or Chinese—*Barbary Coast*) superstition that you can't get to heaven unless you're whole, and Hawks used pain, as he uses other forms of physical experience, to promote an intense spontaneous sympathy between people. The pain in *El Dorado*, starting from the lonely, terrified boy who shoots himself, isolates people rather than drawing them together.

Beside the austerity and rigour of *Rio Bravo*, *El Dorado* seems a colourful, even flamboyant film: there are the extremes of violence and comedy, there are such picturesque details as James Caan's shotgun and Arthur Hunnicutt's bugle and bow-and-arrow; there is the gun-battle in the church, with bells repeatedly rung by being shot at, the altar blasted, bodies falling down the bell-ropes (with one shot—camera underneath, looking up—that, apart from its intrinsically startling quality, comes as a great shock in a Hawks film). For all the colour, however, the big set-pieces come off rather badly if one compares them with their counterparts in *Rio Bravo*. The build-up of the sequence where Wayne and Mitchum follow a wounded man into a saloon, for example, has little of the sustained tension of the blood-in-the-beer scene in the earlier film. It is not *just* a matter of the construction and handling of the sequence: underlying its relatively perfunctory effect—for all the colourful invention of jangling piano and extravagant splinters in the barman's hand, and the comparatively extreme violence—is the fact that we never take Mitchum's alcoholism as seriously as Dude's. The final battle shows the discrepancy even more strikingly. In an obvious attempt to outdo the dynamite fight at the end of *Rio Bravo*, Hawks here throws in everything—Chinaman imitation, bow-and-arrow, shotgun, bugle—and although it is all great fun, one is very much aware of the contrivance, after the spontaneous naturalness of the other film. One can see all this as an attempt to repeat and outdo *Rio Bravo*, and hence decisively recapture a public Hawks may have felt in danger of losing.

Yet there is a way in which it all makes artistic sense—though it is not quite the sense of a self-sufficient work. Hawks is now in his seventies. W. B. Yeats was a few years younger when he wrote

> An aged man is but a paltry thing,
> A tattered coat upon a stick, unless
> Soul clap its hands and sing, and louder sing
> For every tatter in its mortal dress.

The words and imagery suggest at once the need to recapture a childlike, unselfconscious spontaneity, and the contradictory fact that with advancing age attempts to do so will have to be more and more deliberate. In *El Dorado* Hawks is 'singing louder'; there is exactly that balance of recaptured spontaneity and the contradictory sense of deliberateness that Yeats's lines define. And when one realises this, one realises the real subject of the film—a subject virtually all-pervading, yet never stated explicitly: age.

It comes nearest to explicit statement in the opening exchange between Thornton and Harrah. Thornton reaches towards his gun; Harrah warns him off. Thornton: 'I just wanted to see if you'd slowed up any.' Harrah: 'Not that much.' Just before that, Harrah, gun levelled, entered the room where Thornton was washing, and Thornton failed to be aware of him until he spoke. Fear of failing powers, and the desire to compensate for them, pervades the entire film. Despite its superficial appearance of having been motivated by box-office considerations, *El Dorado* is an intensely personal film. Hawks's work since *Rio Bravo* has been widely regarded as evidence of failing powers. The determined boisterousness of *El Dorado*'s manner is clearly reflected in its content. The emphasis

El Dorado: J. P. Harrah and Cole Thornton

throughout is on physical deterioration, not always directly
related to age, but becoming virtually a metaphor for it. Wayne's
attacks of paralysis are the most obvious example: he is seen
clutching his side after *any* exertion, and Hawks makes a great
point of his helplessness on the two occasions of actual collapse
(see his frantic and ignominious struggling to get under a rock
when he hears a horseman coming). The treatment of Mitchum's
alcoholism seems so superficial beside that of Dude's largely
because it is conceived almost entirely in physical terms. In *Rio
Bravo* Hawks used Dude's lack of physical control—his trembling
hands, etc.—consistently to express a spiritual condition; in *El
Dorado* the emphasis is far more on the outward signs of physical
degeneration for their own sake: Harrah's unshaven and bleary
face, the size of his paunch, his stomach-clutching. The 'cure' is
basically physical, too, not moral as in *Rio Bravo*, where there is
no equivalent for Mississippi's horrific concoction of gunpowder
and mustard. The end of the film has Wayne and Mitchum both on

157

crutches. It is not the first time Hawks has treated the subject of age and its problems—one thinks immediately of Thomas Mitchell's failing eyesight in *Only Angels Have Wings*, of Harry Carey in *Air Force*, of Stumpy in *Rio Bravo*—but it is the first time it has been the centre, indeed, the co-ordinating principle, of a Hawks film.

Let us consider the violence of *El Dorado* in a bit more detail. Again, comparison with earlier work is revealing. The moment where Harrah beats Bart Jason in the face with his rifle, close as it is to the saloon scene of *Rio Bravo*, is closer still to the moment in *To Have and Have Not* where Bogart beats Dan Seymour: there is in common not only the beating but the temptation to kill (the trembling hand—'You're a lucky man'—one can also adduce the Matthew/Teeler incident in *Red River*). Action and dialogue are so close as to be almost identical; the difference—a very important one—lies in the motivation of the violence. In *To Have and Have Not* one feels a perfect correspondence between provocation and response. In *El Dorado* the provocation is still there, but it is much less extreme; when one has allowed for it, one still feels something to be accounted for, in the pressures sensed behind the violence. The 'something' is surely age, or physical deterioration: the violence, extreme, almost gratuitous, comes across (whether or not this was the intention—it can be explained quite simply in terms of fashion, Westerns being so much more violent nowadays) as an over-compensation for a vulnerability scarcely found in earlier Hawks heroes. One finds much the same discrepancy between provocation and response if one compares the scene where Thornton drives the gunman out to get shot with its original at the end of *The Big Sleep*. Thornton's sudden paralytic collapse makes the vulnerability clear (and looks very like a stroke or a heart-attack). The same principle underlies the showdown with Nelse Macleod. Nelse is scarcely a 'villain': he is another professional, in the employ of the wrong side, and treated by Wayne (and Hawks) with some respect and sympathy. His death, with its attendant shame at being defeated by a man who lacks the use of his gun-hand, has considerable pathos; it is unpleasantly messy;

and it is the result of a deliberate trick—the only means by which Wayne can win, giving the references to 'professional courtesy' a decidedly ironic quality.

The episode of Luke MacDonald's suicide remains somewhat separate in tone from the rest of the film, but is in many respects a perfectly acceptable prologue. It introduces, with great force, the fact of mortality, and its attendant facts of pain and guilt, pointing forward to the consistently messy, morally impure, or dubious violence later in the film. The innocence of the victim (the later victims of violence are mostly, as it were, professional men who go into things with their eyes open) adds greatly to the intensity of the incident. The scene where Thornton carries Luke's body back to his family is one of the finest examples in Hawks's work of that understating of tragedy that has always been one of its characteristics. The sense of irrevocability is beautifully conveyed.

There are other means in the film of implicitly stressing the heroes' age. There is the curious, seemingly irrelevant, meeting between Wayne and Draper—Sheriff of the town Wayne travels to—the sole purpose of which is to offer an alternative to Wayne's wandering-gunfighter existence: Draper, after a doubtful past, has settled in civilisation, and comparing his life with Wayne's we become more aware of the latter's age. The first appearance of Maudie (Charlene Holt) suggests, significantly, that we are to 'read' the film as *Rio-Bravo*-ten-years-later: Wayne helped her when her gambler-husband got killed, she tells Mitchum, thereby relating herself immediately to Feathers. She is not, however, at all like Feathers: it is much more possible to think of her as a wife in the traditional sense—mainstay of home, raiser of family, cook and housekeeper, etc.—and the film ends with the implication that Wayne is about to retire from his profession and settle down with her. But that is not where the emphasis lies: it is notable that there is no final scene for Wayne and Maudie, to correspond to the ending of *Rio Bravo*—just a somewhat perfunctory statement. Indeed, relationships in *El Dorado* count for surprisingly little. Wayne and Mitchum seem much more separate and isolated than Wayne and Martin (partly, of course, because Harrah is a much less dependent character than Dude; and as usual one cannot separate the characters from the stars here); the men-women relationships, though both have great charm, never develop very far. In *El Dorado* one feels the men—especially the older men—as standing out in isolation against the darkness. Darkness dominates the film. From Thornton's return to El Dorado onwards, there are scarcely any daytime scenes, and what there are are mostly indoors: one's impression is of perpetual night, and the feel of the whole film is affected by this. The lighting of the night scenes, what is more, seems specially designed to bring out a silvery, almost icy quality, particularly in the faces. The darkness surrounding Hawks's world, that I emphasised in discussing *Only Angels Have Wings*, is here felt to be closing in, and its relation to the heroes' age is obvious.

There is no comfort or qualification. The Edgar Allan Poe poem from which the film takes its title might seem to offer some, with its theme of the idealistic search for 'El Dorado' by a 'gallant knight', but its function in the film seems mainly to point by contrast the absence of any El Dorado in the characters' lives—or their hopes. As Wayne says when Mississippi quotes the poem and tells him he's always liked it, ' "Ride, boldly ride"? But it don't turn out that way.' And there is no sign, here or elsewhere in Hawks, of any religious consolation. The gun-battle in the church does not strike one exactly as blasphemous, because the term suggests a deliberate affront to religion. Here one feels that the church is being used simply as a fine dramatic setting for a gunfight, the shattering of the altar (by the *heroes*' bullets) coming across as part of the general uninhibitedness with which the scene is brought off rather than as an attempt to shock religious susceptibilities. This implies, it seems to me, a far more total rejection of Christianity than blasphemy could ever be; it simply means nothing to Hawks, and he has not the slightest qualms about using a church as, in *Rio Bravo*, he uses a farm shed.

Towards the end of the film, when Wayne, despite extreme physical handicaps, is preparing for the final showdown, Mississippi quotes more of the poem:

And when his strength
Failed him at length,
He met a pilgrim shadow,
'Shadow,' said he,
'Where can it be,
This land of El Dorado?'

'Over the mountains of the moon,
Down the valley of the shadow,
Ride, boldly ride,'
The Shade replied,
'If you search for El Dorado.'

Clearly, the 'pilgrim shadow' is as far from finding El Dorado as the knight: there *is* no El Dorado, the film suggests, either in life or in death; there is only the search.

It is profoundly characteristic of Hawks that this film, of which the above account suggests that the keynote should be a black despair, should be among his gayest and funniest works; though the black despair is there too, not very far below the boisterous surface. The tension between black background and gay foreground, in fact, has never before been so extreme. I pointed out, in *Only Angels Have Wings*, the emotional effect of Grant singing the 'Peanut Vendor' in the immediate context of Joe's death, the song becoming a joyous shout of defiance. The gaiety of *El Dorado* has precisely this heroic quality; but it is one thing to show a character doing this in a relatively 'young' work, and quite another to do it yourself in your seventies.

The laughter of *El Dorado*—a spontaneity deliberately recaptured, but none the less genuine for that—calls to mind late Yeats, where one finds a similar co-existence of desperation and heroic gaiety. One thinks, for instance, of the gaiety of *Lapis Lazuli*, with its explicitly stoical quality. In Yeats, of course, there is a perspective one must not look for in Hawks—a perspective given by his feeling for tradition, and for the lost civilisations of the past: Hawks's laughter is heartier, less affected by bitterness, showing greater robustness and blunter sensitivity. There is in *El Dorado* as in late Yeats the same thinness, the same pushing of things to extremes, the same sense of a vitality real enough yet sustained by a deliberate effort of will, in comparison with the wholeness and richness of the works of the later middle period. The time-gap between the 'Tower' volume and 'Last Poems' is almost exactly that between *Rio Bravo* and *El Dorado*, and in terms of the artists' age the parallel is very close. But Hawks, like Yeats, has remained magnificently true to himself.

Appendix: Failures and Marginal Works

Land of the Pharaohs (1955), *Sergeant York* (1941), *The Big Sleep* (1946), *Gentlemen Prefer Blondes* (1953)

Land of the Pharaohs

Hawks disowns *Land of the Pharaohs,* and requested its omission from the retrospective at the National Film Theatre in 1963. He accounts for its failure very simply: 'I didn't know how a Pharaoh talked'; a statement that gives an important clue to Hawks's art. Considered as a compendium of themes abstracted from realisation, *Land of the Pharaohs* is in the mainstream of Hawks's work: a clearly defined group, here the captive race; a young man's development through experience to maturity (Dewey Martin, as in *The Big Sky*); the instant sexual antagonism so common in Hawks's comedies; one can compare the way in which the pyramid comes to obsess the Pharaoh (Jack Hawkins) with John Wayne's obsession with the cattle-drive in *Red River*: for both, once they have embarked on a course of action, it becomes impossible to turn back without losing face, and the films trace the consequent stiffening of the characters into inflexibility.

The film is not devoid of characteristic strengths. One sequence stands out: the building of the pyramid. A panoramic shot reveals the labour in great detail—complicated processes of stone-hewing and stone-heaving: great trouble was taken over authenticity. Hawks resists the temptation to cut in to isolated details, to give impact or to make the most of actions that demanded immense care and cost to stage: what interests him is the complexity of the work-process and he shows it intact, as a vast organism of interacting parts. The complex action is so well organised in relation to the camera's surveyance of it that the spectator grasps it all with perfect clarity. We sense that concern with gettings things right so characteristic of Hawks: one recalls the documentary on lumberjacking in *Come and Get It*, the animal-catching in *Hatari!*. Hawks responds strongly to group effort, whether devoted to building a pyramid or compiling an encyclopedia (*Ball of Fire*). He respects positive achievement and the intelligence and struggle behind it. Indeed, the intelligence and the struggle are more important than the achievement, valued more as their concrete embodiment than for itself. Equally important is the sense of interdependence in group activity. The supreme example of these interests is the rebuilding of the Mary Ann in *Air Force*. Even in *Land of the Pharaohs*, where what is in question is enforced slave labour, the primary response is of admiration for corporate struggle; Hawks shows the work beginning as an act of communal faith—only later does whip supersede work-song.

There is not much more to salvage: some moments expressing a loathing of totalitarianism and its attendant brutalities: the opening triumphal march, with its crude reds and blues garish against the soft grey-yellows of the desert, the mechanical tread of the soldiers over the strewn flowers; the degradation of the slaves building the labyrinth, tongues torn out to prevent them from revealing its secrets, yet abasing themselves before the Pharaoh, showing abject gratitude at his promise of 'pleasures', the total loss of the individual's self-respect.

Hawks 'didn't know how a Pharaoh talked': the few moments worth salvaging consist of general effects, only incidentally related to the narrative. The characters' interchange is so stilted (on whatever level of realism or convention) as to make detailed commentary superfluous. The film as a whole is of value only as a warning to rigid adherents of the *auteur* theory, who assume that a film which is *thematically* characteristic is thereby important. One is entitled to take as evidence of an artist's qualities and interests only work in which he was clearly involved on a personal level, and there is little sign of such involvement in *Land of the Pharaohs*. Various points *might* have been interesting: the Joan Collins character, overtly presented as evil, might have related to the aggressive women in other Hawks films, but in terms of concrete realisation the character is a string of clichés. Where *Land of the Pharaohs* is useful is in the *negative* definition it gives of Hawks's genius: the demonstration (when one places it beside his successes) that his art lives, not on the level of ideas or themes, but in the flesh-and-blood process of *mise-en-scène*, where characters and actors become fused. In theory it ought to be one of Hawks's most important films; but Hawks is the least theoretical of major directors.

Sergeant York

The reasons for the acclamation of *Sergeant York* in 1941 are obvious: its hero, a real-life figure who had captured or killed hundreds of Germans in the First World War while retaining his naïve idealism and remaining at heart a pacifist, seemed to reconcile the most contradictory moral impulses. But the film has retained an underground reputation and the reasons for this are more interesting. Firstly, an aura of respectability hangs around the subject: its truth, in outline at least, is vouched for, and its leading character has all the finest virtues of nobility, sincerity, simplicity, heroism: no other Hawks film has so intrinsically respectable a basis (significantly, it was the only time Hawks has ever been insulted with an Oscar nomination). Secondly, it deals explicitly with important moral issues: the rival claims of religious conviction and patriotic duty. In this it is unique in Hawks's work: the moral implications of his films are implicit in the action, not dealt with as 'issues'. In fact, it is precisely these factors that work consistently against the film's artistic success. One feels Hawks continually hampered by having to 'stick to the facts'; an intuitive artist, he is ill-equipped to handle big issues explicitly on any but a superficial level.

In certain sequences the film springs to life. Alvin's struggle to get the money to buy a piece of 'Bottom Land'—soil more fertile than the rocky hillside ground he forces his plough through—the acquisition of which he believes to be a necessary preliminary to winning Gracie Williams— reveals the essential quality of the Hawks hero: Alvin has set himself a task, and its accomplishment becomes a matter of self-respect. After the turkey-shoot, where he wins the necessary money only to find that the land has already been sold to a rival, Gracie calls to him as he goes off in vengeful desperation, 'Oh Alvin, it don't make no difference'; to which Alvin replies, 'It do to me': the original aim of winning Gracie has been replaced by the need to meet the challenge to his self-respect. It is the film's most characteristic moment. The scenes of work and effort culminating in the turkey-shoot have an intensity and beauty that leave one in no doubt as to the genuineness of Hawks's response, here, to his material. The relationship between York and his mother, based on mutual respect, almost wordless, is realised beautifully and most economically. Alvin comes home after a drinking spree. He stands on the threshold and his mother throws a bucket of water over him. They sit at table, she offers him salt, they smile at each other. Scarcely a word is spoken; the whole relationship is suggested through action, gesture, expression: Alvin's submission to his mother, not dependent or unmanly, deriving from respect for her position and her self; the mother's attitude to her son, not indulging, but *understanding* him, knowing him sufficiently for what he *is* not to be unduly affected by what he *does*.

The sense of community life is very carefully conveyed. Hawks is far more successful here than with the society life of *Come and Get It* or the court of Pharaoh (the only other examples in the adventure films of established communities). Yet paradoxically, in this most 'realist' of Hawks's films one is most uncomfortably aware of the falsifications of

Sergeant York: Alvin and his mother

reality commonly associated with Hollywood. Joan Leslie's Gracie Williams, for example, despite considerable trouble taken in getting her to speak right and look right, remains the Hollywood conception of the country girl. Within the Hollywood conventions, the performance is charming; removed from those conventions, it seems artificial.

In the battle sequences the weakness is more serious. The reconstruction of a First World War battlefield looks authentic; nothing could be less glorious or romantic. Squalor, waste, and uncontrolled confusion are vividly communicated, the complicated action clear to the spectator, however confusing to the participants. But the handling of detail, in character and behaviour, is quite at odds with this. We are jerked abruptly into the world of convention, that convenient agreed shorthand for experience that can so easily degenerate into cliché. There is the death of 'Pusher' (George Tobias), whose peacetime job was to pack people into tube trains at rush-hour, with its inevitable 'End of the line'. Worse in the insensitivity it betrays is the use of Alvin's turkey-gobble noise to induce German soldiers to show their heads. The preceding battle scenes have made death realistically messy and horrible (though it is exclusively the *Americans* who die messily and horribly—the German deaths are clean and painless); then, abruptly, we are invited to

Sergeant York: ploughing

regard killing as a joke—there is no mistaking the tone, and it seems to me distasteful. It is a matter of the level of significance defined by the context. The turkey-gobbling trick would be perfectly acceptable in the climactic gun-battle of *Rio Bravo*, where the conventions operate consistently and where we are never invited to contemplate the pain and horror of violent death: that isn't what the film is about. But it is, partly, what *Sergeant York* is about: York's religion forbids him to kill, and by making American deaths horrible and German deaths perfunctory or funny, Hawks cheats outrageously—the aim was presumably to make it easier for audiences to accept York's subsequent assertion that he did it all to *stop* the killing. But to explain isn't to justify.

The first half of *Sergeant York* is stylistically very beautiful. The compositions, and the quality of the photography, suggest American 'Primitive' painting: see the scenes where Alvin is ploughing and Gracie comes to kiss him, the figures and plough standing out against the skyline; where York, on furlough, sits with his dog on a cliff-ledge to read the American history book lent by his commanding officer; the scene of his conversion. Hawks has sought a style that will express the simplicity of the characters' lives. But, for all its beauty, this in itself suggests the film's limitations: in no film where Hawks is working at full pressure does

'What beautiful photography! What splendid compositions!' occur to one as a first reaction. The externality of the realisation reveals itself most detrimentally in the treatment of religion. The religion depicted is simple and naïve—the presentation of the preacher-storekeeper (Walter Brennan), its chief spokesman, places it quite adequately. It is given a convincingly earthy, rural flavour, expressed in homely parables about finding sows and ploughing round rocks. But if we never feel that we are being asked to accept it, we also never feel that Hawks is particularly engaged by it; Alvin's pacifism, and the religious grounds for it, get only perfunctory treatment, a crippling weakness, as they are inescapably central to the film's subject. The 'Primitive' beauty of the scene where Alvin reads the History of the United States and revelation coincides with sunrise, striking in the simplicity and strength of its imagery, comes across as a means of evading *inward* treatment of Alvin's predicament. The effects of religion on Alvin—his 'Christian' self-abasement before the men who robbed him (morally, if not legally) of his promised 'Bottom Land'—go right against the spirit of Hawks's work, yet Hawks (handicapped no doubt by the facts, and with the real Alvin York still alive) seems not to have had the courage to oppose them firmly: Gracie's spirited attack on Alvin for being unnaturally and distastefully 'noble' carries some weight, but gets lost sight of in the film as a whole. Some critics see it as the tragedy of a man decorated for going against his beliefs: the idea is implicit in the material, but it never reaches adequate realisation. Hawks himself in interviews seems somewhat uncertain about it.

The Big Sleep

The Big Sleep is not exactly a failure, but its success exists within the severest limitations, and the current widespread admiration for it is worth consideration.

On its first appearance it was attacked for violence and amorality. Its reputation has grown out of all proportion to its achievement because of those very qualities that aroused hostility in the forties: violence, cynicism, tough attitudes, 'black' humour are fashionable now, and so is Bogart. Curiously, the real qualities of *The Big Sleep* seem largely to have been overlooked, by attackers and adulators alike.

The question of style and method is crucial. On it depends the great difference between Hawks's film and Chandler's book (which it follows pretty closely in terms of narrative). The book is narrated in the first person by Marlowe, and the reader is restricted throughout—a limitation so confining as to undermine any claims to serious attention made for Chandler—to Marlowe's slick and crude sensibility, which nothing in the book 'places'. We are compelled to see all the characters in Marlowe's terms, and in the language of a cynical arrested adolescent, insisting tiresomely on its own smartness.

At no point and in no way does Hawks attempt a visual equivalent for this style. Nor does he imprison us in Marlowe's consciousness. Robert Montgomery tried to do just that in *Lady in the Lake*, by using subjective camera technique throughout, with Montgomery himself, as Marlowe, only visible when looking in a mirror but in theory present all the time. In theory the spectator became Marlowe/Montgomery. A moment's reflection should have exposed the fallacies, but it's one of those Bright Ideas that a minor talent tends to get hold of and refuse to let go. Far from increasing the sense of spectator-participation the subjective technique was alienating because awkwardly obtrusive. Hitchcock, who commonly encourages audience-identification, never uses subjective techniques in this blatantly literal way. When we look in a mirror, it is not Robert Montgomery's face that looks back; when characters fix us with their eyes and speak straight at us from the screen, apparently expecting us to answer, our reaction is acute selfconsciousness, and we become immediately aware that, whoever we are, we are not Philip Marlowe. When at one point in the film a character punches us (or the camera) in the face, the effect, if crude, is perhaps defensible in communicating Marlowe's surprise: we jump. But we jump even higher later when a character is thrusting his face at us in full close-up through a car window and a fist, theoretically our own, suddenly rises up from the bottom of the screen and punches it on the nose.

Yet even if the subjective technique worked, the result would necessarily be inferior to *The Big Sleep*. For Hawks, unlike Chandler and Montgomery, releases us from Marlowe's consciousness, presenting action and characters (Marlowe included) with his customary objectivity. It is true that every scene begins and ends with Bogart, that we know only what he knows; but we are not forced to see *as* he sees. Besides, what we have is not so much Bogart acting Marlowe as Marlowe becoming Bogart. The ideal Marlowe—from the point of view of fidelity to the original—is Dick Powell in Edward Dmytryk's *Farewell my Lovely*: Powell has exactly the slickness and boyishness, the tough superficiality, of Chandler's Marlowe. Incarnated by Bogart, the character achieves a sympathy and a maturity he never had in the books; placing the smart, cynical remarks as they are never placed by Chandler, making them much less than the expression of the whole man.

Dmytryk repeatedly seeks visual equivalents for Chandler's prose. When Marlowe is knocked out, the comment comes, 'A black pool opened at my feet; I dived in', and the screen fills with ink. Dmytryk's style tends towards Teutonic heaviness, with echoes of German Expressionism in the lighting and special effects, at odds with the Chandlerian slickness without becoming a meaningful comment on it. The *openness* of Hawks's film—

the cool, objective, classical style, editing and camera-movement strictly functional—never oppresses the spectator.

A somewhat negative reason for admiring the film. What, more positively, are the characteristics that transform the atmosphere of Chandler's novel into the subtly different atmosphere of the film? It seems perverse to say it of a film either praised or denounced for its blackness and savagery, a film containing seven (I think) murders and various incidental brutalities; but they are charm and tenderness. Their presence is partly identical with that of Humphrey Bogart, but not entirely explained by it. The film gives us repeatedly, and the book almost never, a sense of positive, sympathetic relationships; in the book the characters merely adopt varyingly 'tough' attitudes towards each other. The mutual affection and respect that develop so naturally between Marlowe and General Sternwood in the opening sequence is barely hinted at in the book, which also offers no equivalent for the tenderness, so simply expressed, between Bogart and the girl in the bookshop (Dorothy Malone). Above all there is the Bogart-Bacall relationship, where, though the dialogue (much of it original Chandler) remains tough and cynical, the acting conveys a mutual sympathetic awareness. The altogether charming and funny little scene where they telephone the police then try to convince whoever is on the other end that *he* was phoning *them* looks like one of those collaborative inspirations of director and players that just grew.

It is also illuminating to set Hawks's film beside Huston's *Maltese Falcon*. Huston's film is more single-minded, the plot clearer: faithful translation of Hammett's novel. Hawks's film is more open. Huston is so determined to explain the plot that there is an inordinate amount of talk: more, even, than in *The Big Sleep*. The treatment of plot in Hawks's film is casual. Hardly anyone can follow it, including apparently Hawks, who maintains that he still doesn't know who committed one of the murders. The film follows Chandler's plot fairly closely until the book's last chapter, then suddenly opts for a different killer. To have Bacall turn out to be the killer would certainly have gone against the whole spirit of the film, but the last-minute switch doesn't make for clarity. Isn't this indifference to plot evidence of Hawks's strength rather than weakness? One respects him for conceiving the film primarily in terms of the Bogart-Bacall relationship, and of Bogart's moral relationship to the background and general atmosphere. While Hammett is superior to Chandler, Hawks is superior to Huston. But the Chandler-Hammett atmosphere is too stifling for Hawks to breathe in happily: he lets in what fresh air he can.

Gentlemen Prefer Blondes

Hawks's out-and-out admirers think particularly highly of *Gentlemen Prefer Blondes*. They are, perhaps, blinded to its shortcomings by their pleasure in recognising the Hawks flavour—a common danger for anyone immersed in an artist's work. *Gentlemen Prefer Blondes* is distinctive without being particularly distinguished: many characteristics of Hawksian comedy are present in a raw state, never fusing into a satisfactory unity. The film lacks any firm positive centre that could give its various elements perspective and make them meaningful.

The brittle, petty humour of Anita Loos's book is incompatible with Hawks's robust and generous comic sense. The material came to Hawks via a Broadway adaptation, already broadened; much of it is thin and banal. Hawks makes it work intermittently by pushing the vulgarity inherent in the character of Lorelei Lee to extremes and allowing it to determine the style. The staging of 'Diamonds are a Girl's Best Friend', with glaring clashes of cerise and scarlet, crude stereotyping of movement and gesture, ghastly human chandeliers and candelabra, expresses the dehumanising effect of Lorelei's money-based, money-obsessed outlook, human beings reduced to objects.

Hawks, in an interview, indicated the film's central weakness, apparently without realising it. 'It was a complete caricature, a travesty on sex. It didn't have normal sex. Jane Russell was supposed to represent sanity.' This self-contradiction is reflected in the Russell character throughout. Hawks conceived her partly as an erotic parallel to Lorelei (Marilyn Monroe): Dorothy collects and devours men for sex as Lorelei for money. This gives us some of the film's sharpest moments, and suggests what it might have been if Hawks had reshaped his material more ruthlessly: a grotesque modern morality, a *reductio ad absurdum* of the contemporary values of money and erotic experience pursued as ends in themselves. The best sequence in the film is the staging of 'Ain't there Anyone Here for Love?' in the ship's gymnasium, with Jane Russell surrounded by the Olympics team too self-absorbed in body-building exercises to notice her. Blank faces and mechanical movements suggest men become machines: the sequence parallels the 'Diamonds' number.

The conception of Dorothy as erotic tigress makes it impossible to take her also as 'representing sanity'; her love scenes with private detective Malone (Elliott Reid), based on commonplace material and played fairly straight, meant to 'place' the relationship of Lorelei and her grotesquely ineffectual millionaire 'lover' (Tommy Noonan), succeed only in being faintly embarrassing. The function of the Russell character changes arbitrarily, and the spectator cannot adjust. Malone seems little more virile than Lorelei's helpless victim, and again one senses confused intentions. The characteristic humiliations imposed on Malone at the hands of the two women (in the film's one really funny scene he is soaked with water, stripped of his trousers, dressed in a feathery negligée, and pushed out into the ship's corridor) quite overshadow any innate dignity

Gentlemen Prefer Blondes: Dorothy with the Olympic athletes

he possesses, making it impossible to take him seriously as an appropriate mate for Dorothy. At moments we take him as a further example of the ineffectual male in a world dominated by women; most of the time he is a conventional musical-comedy hero.

Of all Hawks's films, *Gentlemen Prefer Blondes* is the one most flawed by discrepancies between Hawks's daring originality and the 'safe' conventions of a commercially orientated industry. It contains striking things, but disintegrates under analysis.

Filmography

Howard Hawks

Born Goshen, Indiana, U.S.A. 1896

Studied mechanical engineering at Cornell University, New York

Airman in First World War

Worked in aircraft factory

Began his cinema career as a props man with Mary Pickford Company, then went to the editing department, then to the script department. For some time he was assistant to M. Neilan. He scripted, directed, and financed two comic shorts. He worked on *Tiger Love* (1924) as a script-writer, and wrote the stories for *Dressmaker from Paris* (1925) and *Quicksands* (1926)

Features

The Road to Glory (1926)

Director	Howard Hawks
Script	L. G. Rigby, from story by Hawks
Director of Photography	Joseph August

May McAvoy, Rockliffe Fellows, Leslie Fenton, Ford Sterling.

First shown in U.S.A., 7 February 1926; G.B., 4 October 1926.
Running time, 93 mins.
Distributors: William Fox.

Fig Leaves (1926)

Director	Howard Hawks
Script	Hope Loring, Louis D. Lighton, from story by Hawks
Director of Photography	Joseph August
Costumes	Adrian

George O'Brien, Olive Borden, André de Béranger, Phyllis Haver, Heine Conklin, William Austin.

First shown in U.S.A., 22 August 1926; G.B., 1927.
Running time, 109 mins.
Distributors: William Fox.

The Cradle Snatchers (1927)

Director	Howard Hawks
Script	Sarah Y. Mason, from play by Russell Medcraft and Norma Mitchell
Director of Photography	L. William O'Connell

Arthur Lake, Nick Stuart, Sally Eilers, Louise Fazenda, Ethel Wales, Joseph Striker, Dorothy Phillips.

First shown in U.S.A., 24 April 1927; G.B., 31 October 1927.
Running time, 103 mins.
Distributors: William Fox.

Paid to Love (1927)

Director	Howard Hawks
Script	William M. Conselman, Seton I. Miller, from story by Harry Carr
Director of Photography	L. William O'Connell

Virginia Valli, George O'Brien, William Powell, J. Farrell Macdonald, Thomas Jefferson.

First shown in U.S.A., 15 May 1927; G.B., 28 November 1927.
Running time, 113 mins.
Distributors: William Fox.

A Girl in Every Port (1928)

Director	Howard Hawks
Script	Seton I. Miller, from story by Hawks
Photography	L. William O'Connell, R. J. Berquist
Editor	Ralph Dixon
Titles	Malcolm Stuart Baylan

Victor McLaglen, Robert Armstrong, Louise Brooks, Gretel Yoltz, Natalie Joyce, Maria Casajuana.

First shown in U.S.A., 26 February 1928; G.B., 13 August 1928.
Running time, 97 mins.
Distributors: William Fox.

Fazil (1928)

Director	Howard Hawks
Script	Seton I. Miller, Philip Klein, from play, *L'Insoumise*, by Pierre Frondaie, and the English adaptation, *Prince Fazil*
Director of Photography	L. William O'Connell
Editor	Ralph Dixon

Charles Farrell, Greta Nissen, John Boles, Mae Busch, Tyler Brooke, Eddie Sturgis, Vadim Uraneff, Hank Mann, Josephine Borio.

First shown in U.S.A., 9 September 1928; G.B., 1 October 1928.
Running time, 113 mins.
Distributors: William Fox.

The Air Circus (1928)

Directors	Howard Hawks and Lewis B. Seiler
Script	Seton I. Miller, Norman Z. McLeod, from story by Graham Baker and Andrew Bennison
Director of Photography	Dan Clarke
Editor	Ralph Dixon
Titles	William Kernell
Dialogue	Hugh Herbert

Arthur Lake, Sue Carol, David Rollins, Charles Delaney, Heine Conklin, Louise Dresser, Carl Robinson.

First shown in U.S.A., 30 September 1928; G.B., 18 March 1929.
Running time, 118 mins.
Distributors: William Fox.

Trent's Last Case (1929)

Director	Howard Hawks
Script	Scott Darling, Beulah Marie Dix, from novel by E. C. Bentley
Director of Photography	Harold Rosson
Titles	Malcolm Stuart Baylan

Raymond Griffith, Marceline Day, Raymond Hutton, Lawrence Gray, Donald Crisp, Edgar Kennedy, Nicholas Soussanin, Anita Carvin.

First shown 31 March 1929; G.B., 23 September 1929.
Running time, 96 mins.
Distributors: William Fox.

The Dawn Patrol (1930)

Director	Howard Hawks
Script	Hawks, Don Totheroh, Seton I. Miller, from story, *The Flight Commander*, by John Monk Saunders
Director of Photography	Ernest Haller
Editor	Ray Curtiss

Richard Barthelmess (*Dick Courtney*), Douglas Fairbanks, jun. (*Douglas Scott*), Neil Hamilton (*Major Brand*), William Janney (*Gordon Scott*), James Finlayson (*Field-Sergeant*), Clyde Cook (*Bott*), Gardner James (*Ralph Hollister*), Edmond Breon (*Lieutenant Phipps*), Frank McHugh (*Flaherty*), Jack Ackroyd, Harry Allen (*Mechanics*).

First shown in U.S.A., 10 August 1930; G.B., 16 March 1931.
Running time, 95 mins.
Distributors: First National-Warners.

The Criminal Code (1931)

Producer	Harry Cohn
Director	Howard Hawks
Script	Seton I. Miller, Fred Niblo, jun., from story by Martin Flavin
Director of Photography	James Wong Howe
Editor	Edward Curtis
Recorded by	Glenn Rominger

Walter Huston (*Warden Brady*), Phillips Holmes (*Robert Graham*), Constance Cummings (*Mary Brady*), Mary Doran (*Gertrude Williams*), De Witt Jennings (*Gleason*), John Sheehan (*McManus*), Boris Karloff (*Galloway*), Otto Roffman (*Fales*), Clark Marshall (*Runch*), Arthur Hoyt (*Nettleford*), Ethel Wales (*Katie*), John St Polis (*Dr Rinewulf*), Spelvin (*Paul Porcasi*), Hugh Walker (*Lew*), Jack Vance (*Reporter*).

First shown in U.S.A., 15 January 1931; G.B., 5 October 1931.
Running time, 97 mins.
Distributors: Columbia.

The Crowd Roars (1932)

Director	Howard Hawks
Script	Kubec Glasmon, John Bright, Seton I. Miller, Niven Busch, from story by Hawks
Director of Photography	Sidney Hickox
Editor	John Stumar

James Cagney (*Joe Green*), Joan Blondell (*Anne*), Ann Dvorak (*Lee*), Eric Linden (*Eddie Green*), Guy Kibbee (*Dad Greer*), Frank McHugh (*Spud*), William Arnold (*Bill*), Leo Nomis (*Jim*), Charlotte Merriam (*Mrs Spud Smith*), Harry Hartz, Ralph Hepburn, Fred Guisso, Phil Pardee, Spider Matlock, Jack Brisko, Fred Frame (*Auto Drivers*).

First shown in U.S.A., 16 April 1932; G.B., 26 September 1934.
Running time, 85 mins.
Distributors: Warners.

The Lloyd Bacon remake *Indianapolis Speedway* (1939) includes footage from *The Crowd Roars*.

Scarface (*Shame of a Nation*) (1932)

Production Company	Hughes Production
Producers	Howard Hughes and Hawks
Director	Howard Hawks
Script	Ben Hecht, from novel by Armitage Trail
Adaptation and dialogue	Seton I. Miller, John Lee Mahin, W. R. Burnett
Directors of Photography	Lee Garmes, L. William O'Connell
Editor	Edward Curtis
Music	Adolph Tandler, Gus Arnheim
Sound	William Snyder
Assistant Director	Richard Rosson

Paul Muni (*Tony Camonte*), Ann Dvorak (*Cesca*), Karen Morley (*Poppy*), Osgood Perkins (*Johnny Lovo*), Boris Karloff (*Gaffney*), C. Henry Gordon (*Guarino*), George Raft (*Guino Rinaldo*), Purnell Pratt (*Publisher*), Vince Barnett (*Angelo*), Ines Palange (*Mrs Camonte*), Harry J. Vejar (*Costillo*), Edwin Maxwell (*Chief of Detectives*), Tully Marshall (*Managing Editor*), Henry Armetta (*Pietro*).

First shown in U.S.A., 9 April 1932; G.B., 28 November 1932.
Running time, 90 mins.
Distributors: United Artists.

Tiger Shark (1932)

Director	Howard Hawks
Assistant Director	Richard Rosson
Script	Wells Root, from *Tuna* by Houston Branch
Director of Photography	Tony Gaudio
Editor	Thomas Pratt

Edward G. Robinson (*Mike Mascerena*), Richard Arlen (*Pipes*), Zita Johann (*Quita*), Leila Bennett (*Lady Barber*), Vince Barnett (*Engineer*), J. Carroll Naish (*The Man*), William Ricciardi (*Manuel*).

First shown in U.S.A., 24 September 1932; G.B., 27 February 1933.
Running time, 80 mins.
Distributors: First National-Warners.

Today We Live (1933)

Producer	Howard Hawks
Director	Howard Hawks
Script	Edith Fitzgerald, Dwight Taylor, from story, *Turnabout*, by William Faulkner
Dialogue	William Faulkner
Director of Photography	Oliver T. Marsh
Editor	Edward Curtis

Joan Crawford (*Diana*), Gary Cooper (*Bogard*), Robert Young (*Claude*), Franchot Tone (*Ronnie*), Roscoe Karns (*McGinnis*), Louise Closser Hale (*Applegate*), Rollo Lloyd (*Major*), Hilda Vaughn (*Eleanor*).

First shown in U.S.A., 3 March 1933; G.B., 4 September 1933.
Running time, 113 mins.
Distributors: Metro-Goldwyn-Mayer.

Viva Villa! (1934)

Producer	David O. Selznick
Director	Jack Conway and, uncredited, Howard Hawks
Script	Ben Hecht, from story by Edgcumb Pinchon and O. B. Stade
Photography	James Wong Howe, Charles G. Clarke

Wallace Beery (*Pancho Villa*), Leo Carrillo (*Sierra*), Fay Wray (*Teresa*), Donald Cook (*Don Felipe*), Henry B. Walthall (*Madero*), Joseph Schildkraut (*General Pascal*), Katherine de Mille (*Rosita*), George E. Stone (*Chavito*), Philip Cooper (*Villa as a boy*), Frank Puglia (*Villa's Father*), Francis X. Bushman, jun. (*Calloway*).

First shown in U.S.A., 27 April 1934; G.B., 24 September 1934.
Running time, 115 mins.
Distributors: Metro-Goldwyn-Mayer.

Twentieth Century (1934)

Producer	Howard Hawks
Director	Howard Hawks
Script	Charles MacArthur, Ben Hecht, from their, play, based on play, *Napoleon on Broadway*, by Charles Bruce Milholland
Director of Photography	Joseph August
Editor	Gene Havlick

John Barrymore (*Oscar Jaffe*), Carole Lombard (*Lily Garland*), Walter Connolly (*Webb*), Roscoe Karns (*O'Malley*), Charles Levison (*Jacobs*), Etienne Giradot (*Clark*), Dale Fuller (*Sadie*), Ralph Forbes (*George Smith*), Billie Seward (*Anita*), Clifford Thompson (*Lockwood*), James B. Burtis (*Conductor*), Gi-Gi Parrish (*Schultz*), Edgar Kennedy (*McGonigle*).

First shown in U.S.A., 11 May 1934; G.B., 3 December 1934
Running time, 91 mins.
Distributors: Columbia.

Barbary Coast (1935)

Production Company	Goldwyn Productions
Producer	Samuel Goldwyn
Director	Howard Hawks
Script	Ben Hecht, Charles MacArthur
Director of Photography	Ray June
Editor	Edward Curtis
Music	Alfred Newman

Miriam Hopkins (*Swan*), Edward G. Robinson (*Chamalis*), Joel McCrea (*Carmichael*), Walter Brennan (*Old Atrocity*), Frank Craven (*Col. Cobb*), Brian Donlevy (*Knuckles*), Harry Carey (*Slocum*), Clyde Cook (*Oakie*), J. M. Kerrigan (*Judge Harper*), Donald Meek (*McTavish*), Roger Gray (*Sandy*), Rollo Lloyd (*Wigham*), Matt McHugh (*Bronco*).

First shown in U.S.A., 27 September 1935; G.B., 10 February 1936.
Running time, 91 mins.
Distributors: United Artists.

Ceiling Zero (1935)

Production Company	Cosmopolitan Pictures
Producer	Harry Joe Brown
Director	Howard Hawks
Script	Frank Wead, from his play
Director of Photography	Arthur Edeson
Editor	William Holmes

James Cagney (*Dizzy Davis*), Pat O'Brien (*Jake Lee*), June Travis (*Tommy*), Stuart Erwin (*Texas*), Isabel Jewell, Henry Wadsworth, Craig Reynolds, Richard Purcell, Robert Light, Gary Owen, Barton MacLane, Martha Tibbetts, Edward Garyn, Carlyle Moore, jun., Addison Richards, Pat West, Matilda Comont.

First shown in U.S.A., 25 January 1936; G.B., 26 October 1936.
Running time, 95 mins.
Distributors: First National-Warners.

The Road to Glory (1936)

Producer	Darryl F. Zanuck
Director	Howard Hawks
Script	Joel Sayre, William Faulkner, from the *Wooden Crosses* by Raymond Bernard
Director of Photography	Gregg Toland
Editor	Edward Curtis
Music	Louis Silvers

Fredric March (*Lieutenant Michel Denet*), Warner Baxter (*Captain Paul Laroche*), Lionel Barrymore (*Papa Laroche*), June Lang (*Monique*), Gregory Ratoff (*Bouffiou*), Victor Kilian (*Regnier*), Paul Stanton (*Relief Captain*), John Qualen (*Duflous*), Julius Tannen (*Lieutenant Tannen*), Theodore von Eltz (*Major*), Paul Fix (*Rigaud*), Leonid Kinskey (*Ledoux*), Jacques Lory (*Courier*), Jacques Vernaire (*Doctor*), Edythe Taynore (*Nurse*), George Warrington (*Old Soldier*).

First shown in U.S.A., 2 June 1936; G.B., 8 February 1937.
Running time, 95 mins.
Distributors: Twentieth Century-Fox.

Come and Get It (1936)

Production Company	Goldwyn Productions
Producer	Samuel Goldwyn
Directors	Howard Hawks and William Wyler
Script	Jane Murfin, Jules Furthman, from a novel by Edna Ferber
Photography	Gregg Toland, Rudolph Maté
Editor	Edward Curtis
Music	Alfred Newman

Edward Arnold (*Barney Glasgow*), Joel McCrea (*Richard Glasgow*), Frances Farmer (*Lotta*), Walter Brennan (*Swan Bostrom*), Andrea Leeds (*Evvie Glasgow*), Frank Shields (*Tony Schwerke*), Mady Christians (*Karie*), Mary Nash (*Emma Louise Glasgow*), Clem Bevans (*Gunnar Gallagher*), Edwin Maxwell (*Sid le Maire*).

First shown in U.S.A., 29 October 1936; G.B., 3 May 1937.
Running time, 105 mins.
Distributors: United Artists.

Bringing up Baby (1938)

Producer	Howard Hawks
Associate Producer	Cliff Reid
Director	Howard Hawks
Script	Dudley Nichols, Hager Wilde, from story by Wilde
Director of Photography	Russell Metty
Editor	George Hively
Music	Roy Webb
Art Direction	Van Nest Polglase, Perry Ferguson

Cary Grant (*David Huxley*), Katherine Hepburn (*Susan*), Charles Ruggles (*Major Horace Applegate*), Walter Catlett (*Slocum*), Barry Fitzgerald (*Gogarty*), May Robson (*Aunt Elizabeth*), Fritz Feld (*Dr Lehmann*), Leona Roberts (*Mrs Gogarty*), George Irving (*Peabody*), Tala Birrell (*Mrs Lehmann*), Virginia Walker (*Alice Swallow*), John Kelly (*Elmer*), Asta (*the dog*), Nissa.

First shown in U.S.A., 18 February 1938; G.B., 15 August 1938.
Running time, 102 mins.
Distributors: RKO Radio.

Bringing Up Baby: the dinosaur

Only Angels Have Wings (1939)

Producer	Howard Hawks
Director	Howard Hawks
Script	Jules Furthman, from story by Hawks
Photography	Elmer Dyer, Joseph Walker
Editor	Viola Lawrence
Special Effects	Roy Davidson, Edwin C. Hahn
Music	Dimitri Tiomkin, Morris W. Stoloff

Cary Grant (*Jeff Carter*), Jean Arthur (*Bonnie Lee*), Richard Barthelmess (*Bat McPherson*), Rita Hayworth (*Judith*), Thomas Mitchell (*Kid Dabb*), Sig Ruman (*Dutchman*), Victor Kilian (*Sparks*), John Carrol (*Gent Shelton*), Allyn Joslyn (*Les Peters*), Donald Barry (*Tex Gordon*), Noah Beery, jun. (*Joe Souther*), Melissa Sierra (*Lily*), Lucio Villegas (*Dr Lagorio*), Forbes Murray (*Hartwood*).

First shown in U.S.A., 25 May 1939; G.B., 20 November 1939.
Running time, 121 mins.
Distributors: Columbia.

His Girl Friday (1940)

Producer	Howard Hawks
Director	Howard Hawks
Script	Charles Lederer, from play, *The Front Page*, by Ben Hecht and Charles MacArthur
Director of Photography	Joseph Walker
Editor	Gene Havlick
Music	Morris W. Stoloff

Cary Grant (*Walter Burns*), Rosalind Russell (*Hildy Johnson*), Ralph Bellamy (*Bruce Baldwin*), Gene Lockhart (*Sheriff Hartwell*), Porter Hall (*Murphy*), Ernest Truex (*Bensiger*), Cliff Edwards (*Endicott*), Clarence Kolb (*Mayor*), Roscoe Karns (*McCue*), Frank Jenks (*Wilson*), Regis Toomey (*Sanders*), Abner Biberman (*Diamond Louie*), Frank Orth (*Duffy*), John Qualen (*Earl Williams*), Helen Mach (*Mollie Malloy*), Alma Kruger (*Mrs Baldwin*), Billy Gilbert (*Silas F. Pinkus*).

First shown in U.S.A., 18 January 1940; G.B., 29 July 1940.
Running time, 92 mins.
Distributors: Columbia.

The Outlaw (1940)

Production Company	Hughes Production
Producer	Howard Hughes
Director	Howard Hughes and, uncredited, Howard Hawks
Script	Jules Furthman
Director of Photography	Gregg Toland
Music	Victor Young

Jack Buetel, Jane Russell, Thomas Mitchell, Walter Huston.

First shown U.S.A., 13 February 1943; G.B., 24 February 1947.
Running time, 123 mins.
Distributors: RKO Radio.

Sergeant York (1941)

Producers	Jesse L. Lasky, Hal B. Wallis
Director	Howard Hawks
Script	Abem Finkel, Harry Chandlee, Howard Koch, John Huston, from *War Diary of Sergeant York* edited by Sam K. Cowan, *Sergeant York and His People* by Cowan, *Sergeant York—Last of the Long Hunters* by Tom Skeyhill
Photography	Sol Polito, Arthur Edeson (war sequences)
Editor	William Holmes
Art Direction	John Hughes
Set Direction	Fred MacLean
Music	Max Steiner
Sound	Nathan Levinson

Gary Cooper (*Alvin C. York*), Walter Brennan (*Pastor Rosier Pile*), Joan Leslie (*Gracie Williams*), George Tobias ('*Pusher*' *Rose*), Stanley Ridges (*Major Buxton*), Margaret Wycherley (*Mother York*), Ward Bond (*Ike Botkin*), Noah Beery, jun. (*Buck Lipscomb*), June Lockhart (*Rosie York*), Dickie Moore (*George York*), Clem Bevans (*Zeke*), Howard de Silva (*Lem*), Charles Trowbridge (*Cordell Hull*), Harvey Stevens (*Captain Danforth*), David Bruce (*Bert Thomas*), Charles Esmond (*German Major*), Joseph Sawyer (*Sergeant Early*), Pat Flaherty (*Sergeant Parsons*), Robert Potersfield (*Zeb Andrews*), Erville Alderson (*Nate Tomkins*).

First shown in U.S.A., 9 September 1941; G.B., 9 February 1942.
Running time, 134 mins.
Distributors: Warners.

Ball of Fire (1941)

Production Company	Goldwyn Productions
Producer	Samuel Goldwyn
Director	Howard Hawks
Script	Billy Wilder, Charles Brackett, from story, *From A to Z*, by Wilder and Thomas Monroe
Director of Photography	Gregg Toland
Editor	Daniel Mandell
Art Director	Perry Ferguson
Music	Alfred Newman
Sound	Thomas Moulton

Gary Cooper (*Bertram Potts*), Barbara Stanwyck (*Sugarpuss O'Shea*), Oscar Homolka (*Professor Gurkakoff*), Dana Andrews (*Joe Lilac*), Dan Duryea (*Duke Pastrami*), Henry Travers (*Professor Jerome*), S. Z. Sakall (*Professor Magenbruch*), Tully Marshall (*Professor Robinson*), Leonid Kinskey (*Professor Quintana*), Richard Haydn (*Professor Oddly*), Aubrey Mather (*Professor Peagram*), Allen Jenkins (*Garbage Man*), and Gene Krupa and his Band.

First shown in U.S.A., 9 January 1942; G.B., 18 May 1942.
Running time, 111 mins.
Distributors: RKO Radio (U.S.A.).

Air Force (1943)

Producer	Hal B. Wallis
Director	Howard Hawks
Assistant Director	Jack Sullivan
Script	Dudley Nichols
Dialogue	William Faulkner
Director of Photography	James Wong Howe
Aerial Photography	Elmer Dyer, Charles Marshall
Editor	George Amy
Special Effects	Roy Davidson, Rex Wimpy, H. F. Koenekamp
Chief Pilot	Paul Mantz
Art Director	John Hughes

Set Decorations	Walter F. Tilford
Music	Franz Waxman
Sound	Oliver S. Garretson

John Garfield (*Winocki*), John Ridgely (*Captain Quincannon*), George Tobias (*Corporal Weinberg*), Harry Carey (*Crew Chief*), Edward S. Brophy (*Sergeant in Marines*), Gig Young, Arthur Kennedy, Charles Drake, Ward Wood, Ray Montgomery, James Brown, Stanley Ridges, Willard Robertson, Moroni Olsen, Richard Lane, Bill Crago, Faye Emerson, Addison Richards, James Flavin, Ann Doran, Dorothy Peterson.

First shown in U.S.A., 20 March 1943; G.B., 28 June 1943.
Running time, 124 mins.
Distributors: Warners

Corvette K–225 (The Nelson Touch) (1943)

Producer	Howard Hawks
Director	Richard Rosson
Script	Lieutenant John Rhodes Sturdy, RCNVR
Photography	Tony Gaudio, Harry Perry
Editor	Edward Curtis

Randolph Scott, Ella Raines, James Brown, Barry Fitzgerald, Andy Devine, Fuzzy Knight, Noah Beery, jun., Richard Lane, Thomas Gomez.

First shown in U.S.A., 1 October 1943; G.B., 24 April 1944.
Running time, 99 mins.
Distributors: Universal.

To Have and Have Not (1944)

Producer	Howard Hawks
Director	Howard Hawks
Assistant Director	Jack Sullivan
Script	Jules Furthman, William Faulkner, from the novel by Ernest Hemingway
Director of Photography	Sidney Hickox
Editor	Christian Nyby
Art Director	Charles Novi
Set Decorations	Casey Roberts
Songs	Hoagy Carmichael, Johnny Mercer

187

The Big Sleep: Bacall and Bogart

Music	Leo F. Forbstein
Special Effects	Roy Davidson, Rex Wimpy
Technical Adviser	Louis Comien
Sound	Oliver S. Garretson

Humphrey Bogart (*Harry Morgan*), Walter Brennan (*Eddie 'The Rummy'*), Lauren Bacall (*Slim*), Dolores Moran (*Helène de Bursac*), Hoagy Carmichael (*Crickett*), Walter Molnar (*Paul de Bursac*), Sheldon Leonard (*Lieutenant Coyo*), Marcel Dalio (*Frenchy*), Walter Sande (*Johnson*), Dan Seymour (*Captain Renard*), Aldo Nadi (*Bodyguard*), Paul Marion (*Beauclerc*), Patricia Shay (*Mrs Beauclerc*), Pat West (*Bartender*), Emmet Smith (*Emil*).

First shown in U.S.A., 20 January 1945; G.B., 16 July 1945.
Running time, 100 mins.
Distributors: Warners.

The Big Sleep (1946)

Producer	Howard Hawks
Director	Howard Hawks

Assistant Director	Chuck Hansen
Script	William Faulkner, Leigh Brackett, Jules Furthman, from the novel by Raymond Chandler
Director of Photography	Sidney Hickox
Editor	Christian Nyby
Music	Max Steiner
Art Director	Carl Jules Weyl
Set Decorations	Fred M. MacLean
Special Effects	Roy Davidson, Warren E. Lynch
Sound	Robert B. Lee

Humphrey Bogart (*Philip Marlowe*), Lauren Bacall (*Vivian*), John Ridgely (*Eddie Mars*), Martha Vickers (*Carmen*), Dorothy Malone (*Bookshop Girl*), Peggy Knusden (*Mona Mars*), Regis Toomey (*Bernie Ohls*), Charles Waldren (*General Sternwood*), Charles D. Brown (*Norris*), Bob Steele (*Canino*), Elisha Cook, jun. (*Jones*), Louis Jean Heydt (*Joe Brody*), Sonia Darrin (*Agnes*), Theodore von Eltz (*Geiger*), Tom Rafferty (*Carol Lundgren*).

First shown in U.S.A., 31 August 1946; G.B., 21 October 1946.
Running time, 114 mins.
Distributors: Warners.

Red River (1948)

Production Company	Monterey Productions
Producer	Howard Hawks
Director	Howard Hawks
Assistant Director	Arthur Rosson
Script	Borden Chase, Charles Schnee, from novel, *The Chisholm Trail*, by Chase
Director of Photography	Russell Harlan
Editor	Christian Nyby
Music	Dimitri Tiomkin
Art Director	John Datu Arensma

John Wayne (*Tom Dunson*), Montgomery Clift (*Matthew Garth*), Joanne Dru (*Tess Millay*), Walter Brennan (*Groot*), Coleen Gray (*Fen*), John Ireland (*Cherry*), Noah Beery, jun. (*Buster*), Chief Yowlachie (*Quo*), Harry Carey, sen. (*Melville*), Harry Carey jun. (*Dan Latimer*), Mickey Kuhn (*Matthew as a boy*), Paul Fix (*Teeler*), Hank Warden (*Sims*),

Red River: crossing the Red River

Ivan Parry (*Bunk Kenneally*), Hal Taliaferro (*Old Leather*), Paul Fiero (*Fernandez*), Billy Self, Ray Hyke.

First shown in U.S.A., 20 August 1948; G.B., 1948.
Running time, 125 mins.
Distributors: United Artists.

A Song is Born (1948)

Production Company	Goldwyn Productions
Producer	Samuel Goldwyn
Director	Howard Hawks
Script	Harry Tugent
Director of Photography	Gregg Toland
Songs	Don Raye, Gene DePaul
Editor	Daniel Mandell

Danny Kaye (*Professor Robert Frisbee*), Virginia Mayo (*Honey Swanson*), Benny Goodman (*Professor Magenbruch*), Hugh Herbert (*Professor Twingle*), Steve Cochrane (*Tony Crow*), J. Edward Bomberg (*Dr Elfini*),

Felix Bressart (*Professor Gurkakoff*), Ludwig Stossel (*Professor Traumer*), O. Z. Whitehead (*Professor Oddly*), Esther Dale (*Miss Bragg*), Mary Field (*Miss Totten*), and Tommy Dorsey, Louis Armstrong, Lionel Hampton, Charlie Barnett, Mel Powell, Buck and Bubbles, The Page Cavanagh Trio, The Golden Gate Quartet, and Russo and the Samba Kings.

First shown in U.S.A., 6 November 1948; G.B., 17 October 1949.
Running time, 113 mins.
Distributors: RKO Radio.

I Was a Male War Bride (You Can't Sleep Here) (1949)

Producer	Sol C. Siegel
Director	Howard Hawks
Assistant Director	Arthur Jacobson
Script	Charles Lederer, Leonard Spigelgass, Hagar Wilde, from novel by Henri Rochard
Photography	Norbert Brodine, O. H. Borradaile
Editor	James B. Clark
Art Directors	Lyle Wheeler, Albert Hogsett
Set Decorations	Thomas Little
Music	Cyril Mockridge
Sound	George Leverett, Roger Heman

Cary Grant (*Henri Rochard*), Ann Sheridan (*Catherine Gates*), William Neff (*Captain Jack Rumsey*), Eugene Gericke (*Tony Jowitt*), Marion Marshall, Randy Stuart (*Waacs*), Ruben Wendorf (*Innkeeper's Assistant*), Lester Sharpe (*Waiter*), Ken Tobey (*Seaman*), Robert Stevenson (*Lieutenant*), Alfred Londer (*Bartender*), David McMahon (*Chaplain*), Joe Haworth (*Shore Patrol*).

First shown in U.S.A., September 1949; G.B., 14 November 1949.
Running time, 105 mins.
Distributors: Twentieth Century-Fox.

The Thing (from Another World) (1951)

Production Company	Winchester Productions
Producer	Howard Hawks
Associate Producer	Edward Lasker
Director	Christian Nyby

Assistant Directors	Arthur Siteman, Max Henry
Script	Charles Lederer, from story, *Who Goes There*, by John Wood Campbell, jun.
Director of Photography	Russell Harlan
Editor	Roland Cross
Music	Dimitri Tiomkin
Art Director	Albert S. D'Agostino
Set Decorations	Darrell Silvera, William Stevens
Special Effects	Linwood Dunn, Donald Steward
Sound	Phil Brigandi, Clem Portman

Margaret Sheridan (*Nikki*), Kenneth Tobey (*Captain Patrick Hendrey*), Robert Cornthwaite (*Professor Carrington*), Douglas Spencer (*Skeely*), James Young (*Lieutenant Eddie Dykes*), Dewey Martin (*Crew Chief*), Robert Nichols (*Lieutenant Ken Erickson*), William Self (*Colonel Barnes*), Eduard Franz (*Dr Stern*), Sally Creighton (*Mrs Chapman*), James Arness (*The Thing*).

First shown in U.S.A., April 1951; G.B., 10 November 1951.
Running time, 87 mins.
Distributors: RKO Radio.

The Big Sky (1952)

Production Company	Winchester Productions
Producer	Howard Hawks
Director	Howard Hawks
Assistant Director	Arthur Rosson
Script	Dudley Nichols, from novel by A. B. Guthrie, jun.
Director of Photography	Russell Harlan
Editor	Christian Nyby
Music	Dimitri Tiomkin
Art Direction	Albert S. D'Agostino, Perry Ferguson
Set Decorations	Darrell Silvera, William Stevens

Kirk Douglas (*Jim Deakins*), Dewey Martin (*Boone*), Elizabeth Threatt (*Teal Eye*), Arthur Hunnicutt (*Zeb*), Buddy Baer (*Romaine*), Steven Geray (*Jourdonnais*), Hank Worden (*Poordevil*), Jim Davis (*Streak*), Henri Letondal (*Labadie*), Robert Hunter (*Chouquette*), Booth Colman (*Pascal*), Paul Frees (*McMasters*), Frank de Cova (*Moleface*), Guy Wilkerson (*Longface*).

First shown in U.S.A., August 1952; G.B., 8 December 1952.
Running time, 140 mins.
Distributors: RKO Radio.

O. Henry's Full House (Full House) (1952)

Five-part omnibus film, based on stories by O. Henry, produced by
André Hakim. *The Ransom of Red Chief* episode directed by Howard
Hawks.

Script	Nunnally Johnson
Director of Photography	Milton Krasner

Fred Allen (*Sam*), Oscar Levant (*Bill*), Lee Aaker (*J.B.*), Kathleen
Freeman (*J.B.'s mother*).

First shown in U.S.A., September 1952; G.B., 10 November 1952.
Running time, approximately 20 mins.
Distributors: Twentieth Century-Fox.

Monkey Business (1952)

Producer	Sol C. Siegel
Director	Howard Hawks
Script	Ben Hecht, I. A. L. Diamond, and Charles Lederer, from story by Harry Segall
Director of Photography	Milton Krasner
Editor	William B. Murphy
Music	Leigh Harline
Art Directors	Lyle Wheeler, George Patrick
Set Decorations	Thomas Little, Walter M. Scott

Cary Grant (*Professor Barnaby Fulton*), Ginger Rogers (*Edwina Fulton*),
Charles Coburn (*Oliver Oxly*), Marilyn Monroe (*Lois Laurel*), Hugh
Marlowe (*Hank Entwhistle*), Henri Letondal (*Dr Siegfried Kitzel*),
Robert Cornthwaite (*Dr Zoldeck*), Larry Keating (*G. J. Gulverly*),
Douglas Spencer (*Dr Bruner*), Esther Dale (*Mrs Rhinelander*), George
Winslow (*Deep-voiced boy*), Emmett Lynn (*Jimmy*).

First shown in U.S.A., September 1952; G.B., 6 October 1952.
Running time, 97 mins.
Distributors: Twentieth Century-Fox.

Gentlemen Prefer Blondes

Gentlemen Prefer Blondes (1953)

Producer	Sol C. Siegel
Director	Howard Hawks
Script	Charles Lederer, from play by Anita Loos, Joseph Fields
Director of Photography	Harry J. Wild
Colour Process	Technicolor
Editor	Hugh S. Fowler
Songs	Jule Styne, Leo Robin, Hoagy Carmichael, Harold Adamson
Art Directors	Lyle Wheeler, Joseph C. Wright

Jane Russell (*Dorothy*), Marilyn Monroe (*Lorelei*), Charles Coburn (*Sir Francis Beekman*), Elliott Reid (*Malone*), Tommy Noonan (*Gus Esmond*), George Winslow (*Henry Spofford III*), Marcel Dalio (*Magistrate*), Taylor Holmes (*Esmond, sen.*), Norma Varden (*Lady Beekman*), Howard Wendell (*Watson*), Steven Geray (*Hotel Manager*), Henry Letondal (*Grotier*), Leo Mostovoy (*Philippe*).

First shown in U.S.A., August 1953; G.B., 1 March 1954.
Running time, 91 mins.
Distributors: Twentieth Century-Fox.

Land of the Pharaohs (1955)

Producer	Howard Hawks
Associate Producer	Arthur Siteman
Director	Howard Hawks
Script	William Faulkner, Harry Kurnitz, Harold Jack Bloom
Photography	Lee Garmes, Russell Harlan
Colour Process	Warner Colour
Supervising Editor	Rudi Fehr
Editor	V. Sagovsky
Music	Dimitri Tiomkin
Art Director	Alexandre Trauner
Costumes	Mayo

Jack Hawkins (*Pharaoh*), Joan Collins (*Princess Nellifer*), Dewey Martin (*Senta*), Alexis Minotis (*Hamar*), James Robertson Justice (*Vashtar*), Luisa Boni (*Kyra*), Sydney Chaplin (*Treneh*), James Hayter (*Vashtar's servant*), Kerima (*Queen Nailla*), Piero Giagnoni (*Pharaoh's son*).

First shown in U.S.A., 2 July 1955; G.B., 5 February 1956.
Running time, 106 mins.
Distributors: Warners.

Rio Bravo (1959)

Production Company	Armada Productions
Producer	Howard Hawks
Director	Howard Hawks
Assistant Director	Paul Helmick
Script	Jules Furthman, Leigh Brackett, from story by B. H. McCampbell
Director of Photography	Russell Harlan
Colour Process	Technicolor
Editor	Folmar Blangsted
Music	Dimitri Tiomkin
Songs	Tiomkin, Paul Francis Webster
Art Director	Leo K. Kuter
Set Decorations	Ralph S. Hurst
Costumes	Marjorie Best
Sound	Robert B. Lee

John Wayne (*John T. Chance*), Dean Martin (*Dude*), Ricky Nelson (*Colorado*), Angie Dickinson (*Feathers*), Walter Brennan (*Stumpy*), Ward Bond (*Pat Wheeler*), John Russell (*Nathan Burdett*), Pedro Gonzalez-Gonzalez (*Carlos*), Estelita Rodriguez (*Consuela*), Claude Akins (*Joe Burdett*), Harry Carey, jun. (*Harold*), Malcolm Atterbury (*Jake*), Bob Steele (*Matt Harris*).

First shown in U.S.A., 4 April 1959; G.B., 20 July 1959.
Running time, 141 mins.
Distributors: Warners.

Hatari! (1962)

Production Company	Malabar Productions
Producer	Howard Hawks
Director	Howard Hawks
Assistant Directors	Tom Connors, Russ Saunders
Associate Producer and Second Unit Director	Paul Helmick
Script	Leigh Brackett, from story by Harry Kurnitz
Director of Photography	Russell Harlan
Associate Photographer	Joseph Brun
Colour Process	Technicolor
Editor	Stuart Gilmore
Art Direction	Hal Pereira, Carl Anderson
Set Decorations	Sam Comer, Claude E. Carpenter
Special Effects	John P. Fulton
Music	Henry Mancini
Costumes	Edith Head, Frank Beetson, jun.
Sound	John Carter, Charles Grenzbach
Technical Adviser	Willy deBeer

John Wayne (*Sean Mercer*), Elsa Martinelli (*Dallas*), Hardy Kruger (*Kurt Mueller*), Gérard Blain (*Chips Maurey*), Red Buttons (*Pockets*), Michèle Girardon (*Brandy*), Bruce Cabot (*Indian*), Valentin de Vargas (*Luis*), Eduard Franz (*Dr Sanderson*),

First shown in U.S.A., June 1962; G.B., 18 February 1963.
Running time, 159 mins.
Distributors: Paramount.

Man's Favourite Sport? (1963)

Production Company	Gibraltar/Laurel. A Howard Hawks Production
Producer	Howard Hawks
Director	Howard Hawks
Assistant Director	Tom Connors, jun.
Script	John Fenton Murray, Steve McNeil. Based on a story, *The Girl Who Almost Got Away*, by Pat Frank
Director of Photography	Russell Harlan
Colour Process	Technicolor
Editor	Stuart Gilmore
Music	Henry Mancini
Art Directors	Alexander Golitzen, Tambi Larsen
Special Effects	Ben MacMahon
Sound	Waldon O. Watson, Joe Lapis

Rock Hudson (*Roger Willoughby*), Paula Prentiss (*Abigail Page*), Maria Perschy (*Isolde 'Easy' Mueller*), John McGiver (*William Cadwalader*), Charlene Holt (*Tex Connors*), Roscoe Karns (*Major Phipps*), James Westerfield (*Policeman*), Norman Alden (*John Screaming Eagle*), Forrest Lewis (*Skaggs*), Regis Toomey (*Bagley*), Tyler McVey (*Customer Bush*), Kathie Brown (*Marcia*).

First shown in U.S.A., March 1964; G.B., 3 May 1964.
Running time, 127 mins.
Distributors: Rank/Universal International.

Red Line 7000 (1965)

Production Company	Laurel
Producer	Howard Hawks
Director	Howard Hawks
Second Unit Director	Bruce Kessler
Assistant Director	Dick Moder
Script	Howard Hawks, George Kirgo
Director of Photography	Milton Krasner
Colour Process	Technicolor
Editors	Stuart Gilmore, Bill Brame
Music	Nelson Riddle
Art Directors	Hal Pereira, Arthur Lonergan
Special Effects	Paul K. Lerpae
Sound	Keith Stafford

James Caan (*Mike Marsh*), Laura Devon (*Julie Kazarian*), Gail Hire (*Holly MacGregor*), Charlene Holt (*Lindy Bonaparte*), John Robert Crawford (*Ned Arp*), Marianna Hill (*Gabrielle Queneau*), James Ward (*Dan McCall*), Norman Alden (*Pat Kazarian*), George Takei (*Kato*), Diane Strom, Anthony Rogers, Carol Connors, Cissy Wellman.

First shown in U.S.A., 1965; G.B., 11 November 1966.
Running time, 127 mins.
Distributors: Paramount.

El Dorado (1966)

Production Company	Paramount/Laurel
Producer	Howard Hawks
Director	Howard Hawks
Assistant Director	Andrew J. Durkus
Script	Leigh Brackett. Based on the novel *The Stars in their Courses* by Harry Brown
Director of Photography	Harold Rosson
Colour Process	Technicolor
Editor	John Woodcock
Music	Nelson Riddle
Art Directors	Hal Pereira, Carl Anderson
Sound	John Carter, Charles Grenzbach

John Wayne (*Cole Thornton*), Robert Mitchum (*J. P. Harrah*), James Caan (*Alan Bourdillon Traherne, called Mississippi*), Charlene Holt (*Maudie*), Michele Carey (*Joey MacDonald*), Arthur Hunnicutt (*Bull Harris*), R. G. Armstrong (*Kevin MacDonald*), Edward Asner (*Bart Jason*), Paul Fix (*Doc Miller*), Christopher George (*Nelse Mcleod*), Robert Donner (*Milt*), John Gabriel (*Pedro*), Jim Davis (*Jason's Foreman*), Marina Ghane (*Maria*), Anne Newman (*Saul MacDonald's Wife*), Johnny Crawford (*Luke MacDonald*), Robert Rothwell (*Saul MacDonald*), Adam Roarke (*Matt MacDonald*), Charles Courtney (*Jared MacDonald*), Diane Strom (*Matt's Wife*), Victoria George (*Jared's Wife*), Anthony Rogers (*Dr Donavan*), Olaf Wieghorst (*Swedish Gunsmith*).

First shown in U.S.A., June 1967; G.B., 6 August 1967.
Running time, 110 mins.
Distributors: Paramount.

Red Line 7000: Holly, Gaby and Dan

Acknowledgements

I want to acknowledge a general indebtedness to the criticism of Dr F. R. Leavis. There is no question of *direct* influence (I should be surprised to learn that Dr Leavis had ever heard of Howard Hawks); but I feel that any strength this book may be felt to have derives from the basis of critical values that Dr Leavis's work has given me.

I am grateful to Mr Ib Monty of the Danish Film Archive, Copenhagen, and to Mr Frank Holland of the British Film Archive, Aston Clinton, for making it possible for me to see various Hawks films that are otherwise unavailable, and for their extreme kindness and hospitality during my visits; and to the Stockholm Film School for inviting me to a private screening of *To Have and Have Not*.

Certain parts of this book have been developed from articles that appeared in *Movie, Chaplin, Focus*, and the Welwyn Garden City High School Film Society Bulletin, and I am grateful to the editors for their encouragement.

Stills are reproduced by courtesy of Twentieth Century-Fox, Paramount, Columbia, Warners, RKO Radio, Grand National, New Realm, Ritz, and United Artists.

Too many personal friends, acquaintances and students have influenced my text in small ways (whether in conversation or classroom discussion) for it to be possible to name them, but I am certainly aware of how valuable their remarks have been to me. Peter Wollen has had a particular influence on the chapter on *El Dorado*. From my students I must single out David Moran, who has been closely associated with this book from the outset, who has seen more Hawks films with me and discussed them more than anyone else besides my wife, and whose criticisms of Hawks have caused me to think or re-think many points; I dedicate the book to him.

R. W.